By Hugo Dunn-Meynell and Norman Riley
A Wine Record

The Wine & Food Society Menu Book

By Hugo Dunn-Meynell and Norman Riley
A Wine Record

The Wine & Food Society Menu Book

To Harry Yoxall
and Alice and Pierre Salmon
with our love

This book is a publication of the International Wine & Food Society. Founded by the late André L. Simon in 1933, the Society has members all over the world. It publishes its own Journal, offers merchandise related to civilised eating and drinking, and provides information to its members on gastronomic subjects. Through its branches in many countries, it organises wine tastings, meals, lectures, demonstrations, and tours for the benefit of its members.

Details of membership can be obtained from The Director General, The International Wine & Food Society, 66 Wells Street, London W1P 3RB, England. Telephone: 01-637-2895.

Contents

Foreword

Every once in a while a newspaper with a little too much air in its columns asks its readers to send in their favourite words. My submission (or one of them) would be "celebration". I like the fact, of course, and the flying corks. I also feel the resonance of the word that links champagne and the Sacrament – just as André Simon, life-long celebrant in both senses, did and taught me to do.

André Simon founded what is now the International Wine & Food Society fifty years ago, in a time of dole and dearth, as a practical demonstration that discriminating taste can make a feast from only meagre ingredients. When the Society was thirty years old, I had the good fortune to serve it as Secretary and editor of its journals under André's direct guidance – patronage that I cannot have deserved but have (literally) dined out on ever since. It seems yesterday that we sat together in his big library overlooking Hyde Park, plotting a dinner at the Savoy or lunch in the country. "Sit where you can keep an eye on the waiters," said André. (A looking-glass was always helpful in checking that only empty bottles found their way out behind the screens into the kitchen.)

Fifty years of good fellowship, good wines and good fare in a brotherhood that stretches round the world; this is the legacy which this book celebrates. It also encapsulates fifty years of experience from an astonishing variety of authoritative sources. It is a treasury of what the Society has long called Memorable Meals – complete with instructions. You need turn no further than to the Contents page to see that this is no ordinary cookbook. "Game for two" may not mean quite what it suggests, but each episode from "Luncheon with the French" through

ix

"Grandfather's egg" to "Late supper, wild mushrooms" is a story, a menu and a method – a marvellous way of stimulating interest and appetite, then, as you might say, of spilling the beans.

Alice Salmon has turned the potential chaos of an international cookbook into order and calm, interpreting each recipe with experience and authority.

Hugo Dunn-Meynell speaks with both wisdom and wit about the wines.

What is especially refreshing, and convincing, about their anthology is the sense of practical reality that pervades it. These meals work, are fun, and have been recorded in all their detail. There are special and individual celebrations here – but a *sense* of celebration pervades all.

In 1933, André wrote *Tables of Content*, recreating the atmosphere of meals he had most enjoyed, and sixteen years later his classic, *In Praise of Good Living*. This book reminds me wonderfully of those. André's Society is alive and well, with a bigger parish than ever.

Hugh Johnson

Acknowledgements

We would like to make the following acknowledgements for permission to reproduce material used here:

The Condé Nast Publications Ltd., London, for extracts from "Wine Days" (*Vogue*, July 1982) by H. W. Yoxall; and for five recipes originally published in *House & Garden* by Alice Wooledge Salmon.

The Macmillan Press Ltd., London, for the recipe *rava* from *Understanding Cookery* by Jenny Kavarana, first published 1979.

Essen & Trinken, Hamburg, West Germany, for the recipe *soufflé glacé aux canneberges* by Lyn Hall, published March 1980.

Patrick Forbes for an extract from *Champagne: The Wine, The Land and The People*, published by Victor Gollancz Ltd., London, 1979.

George Rainbird and Michael Joseph Ltd, London, for the recipe 'plum chutney' from *Cooking With Joy* by Joy Rainbird, first published 1971.

A list of contributors and testers of recipes

Karen Celeste Aborjaily, Boston, Massachussets; Rosaline Aikman, Guernsey, Channel Islands; Mary B. Allen, Columbus, Ohio; Colman Andrews, Alta, California; Mary Atkinson, Boston, Massachussets.

Sam Baldone, Columbus, Ohio; Maria Beldekas, Boston, Massachussets; Helene Bennett, New York; Jeffery Benson, London; Sandy Bibby, Hiraethog, Wales; Brad Blakeman, Northern Illinois; Aaron Bloom, New York; Mrs Aaron Bloom, New York; Michel Bourdin, London; Mrs P. Bradbury; Robert L. Brintnell, Windsor, Ontario; John J. Brogan, Palm Beach, Florida; Joseph L. Broosky, Alta, California; Lee M. Brown, Windsor, Ontario; John Charles Bruno, New York; Mary Butt, Rochester, Minnesota.

Elizabeth Charpie, Boston, Massachussets; Joan Chenhalls, London; Tom Childs, Auckland, New Zealand; Carole Collier, New York; Tess Collins, Limerick, Ireland; Joan Copel, Northern Illinois; Roger Copel, Northern Illinois; Mark B. Coventry, Rochester, Minesota; Marion Cunningham, Melbourne, Australia; Olive Cusack, Limerick, Ireland; René Cusack, Limerick, Ireland.

Felicity Davies, Regina, Saskatchewan; Stanley Davies, Regina, Saskatchewan; Martin A. Denni, South Bay, California; Peter Devereux, Johannesburg; Carol Digges, Palm Beach, Florida; Sam Digges, Palm Beach, Florida; Elizabeth A. Di Loreto, Boston, Massachussets; Margaretta S. Drake, Chicago, Illinois; Crispin Dunn-Meynell, London; Nadine Dunn-Meynell, Brentford, Middlesex, England.

Dorothy Ellis, London; Geoffrey Ellis, London; Herbert Engelbert, Philadelphia, Pennsylvania; Len Evans, Sydney, Australia.

Lesley Faull, Rondebosch, South Africa; Patrick Forbes, London; Ron Franklin, Sydney, Australia; Sandra Franklin, Sydney, Australia; Gladys Furness, London; Mary J. Furness, London.

Dorothy Gibson, Melbourne, Australia; Lorraine Gillespie, Edmonton, Alberta; R. Gilmore, Auckland, New Zealand; Lise B. Graves, London; Sid Greenberg, Alta, California.

Lyn P. Hall, Richmond, Surrey, England; Wendy Hall, London; Hilary Halpin, London; Joan W. Hamilton, Honolulu, Hawaii; Robert E. Hamilton, Honolulu, Hawaii; John A. I. Hayward, London; Kathleen E. Helmer, Calgary, Alberta; Michael A. J. Hince, Victoria, Australia; Sue Hinsdale, Palm Beach, Florida; Barbara D. Holland, Columbus, Ohio; Robert J. Holland, Columbus, Ohio; David A. Holtom, London; S. Hiang Holtom, London; Martha Holzapfel; Mrs M. L. Hulton, London.

Patricia Ingle-Finch, Aberdeen, Scotland.

Thelma Jackson, Northampton, England; David Jones, Tokyo; Virginia Jones, Tokyo; Barbara Joyce, Melbourne, Australia; Peter Joyce, Melbourne, Australia.

Lindsay Karnovsky, Johannesburg; Syd Karnovsky, Johannesburg; Bomi Kavarana, Surrey, England; Jenny Kavarana, Surrey, England; Anne Kidd, East Lothian, Scotland; Maurice Kidd, East Lothian, Scotland; Sadelle Koppel, Northern Illinois.

Maryalice Laforest, St. Petersburg, Florida; Harriet Lembeck, New York; William Lembeck, New York; Mabel Lloyd Hughes, Hiraethog, Wales; Frank Lloyd Wright Jr., Washington; Betty Long, Surrey Hills, England; John Long, Surrey Hills, England; Lady Patricia Lousada, London; Count Alexandre de Lur Saluces, Sauternes, Bordeaux.

Bonnie McConnell, Northern Illinois; David E. McConnell, Northern Illinois; Ernine McDermot, Limerick, Ireland; Christopher W. McDonald, Tokyo; Maureen McMahon, Limerick, Ireland; Carol McMullen, Boston, Massachussets; Richard S. McQuown, Pittsburgh, Pennsylvania; Ronald P. Mahoney, Houston, Texas; Alize Malan, Worcester, South Africa; Pat Marshall, Melbourne, Australia; Mollie Matthews, London; Patrick Matthews, London; Sarah Matthews, Paris; Peg May, Northern Illinois; Howard Meighan, New York; Louise

Millison, New York; Helen Mills, Surrey, England; Nancy Minor-Denni, South Bay, California; Guy Mouilleron, London.

James A. Nassikas, Marin County, California; Mrs M. Newnes, Northampton, England; Carole Nimelstein, Marin County, California; Raymond H. Norlin, Northern Illinois; Haskell F. Norman, Marin County, California; Rachel H. Norman, Marin County, California.

Eugene O'Brien, Northern Illinois; H. A. Olsen, Tokyo; Stanley Oleksiuk, Windsor, Ontario; Raelyn Ossipoff, Honolulu, Hawaii; Vladimir Ossipoff, Honolulu, Hawaii; Joe O'Byrne, Limerick, Ireland; Anne O'Sullivan, Limerick, Ireland.

Perrine Palmer, Miami, Florida; F. Clive de Paula, London; Dodie Pickup, Mid-Cheshire, England.

George Rainbird, London; Anne Reves, Chicago; Colin G. Reynolds, Stockport, Cheshire, England; Leslie Richfield, Johannesburg; Tricia Rocke, Basingstoke, Hampshire, England; Pamela Rogers, London; James S. Rossbach, New York; Joy Fontes Rothwell, Lancashire, England and Houston, Texas.

Alice Stürcke Salmon, Hillsborough, California; Caryl Saunders, Marin County, California; Elvira M. Serra, Columbus, Ohio; Ralph J. Serra, Columbus, Ohio; Robert D. Shack, New York; Mrs M. Sharp, Northern Illinois; Maggie Sharp, Surrey, England; Esther Shaw, Calgary, Alberta; Louis C. Skinner, Jr., Miami, Florida; Carole I. Smith, Calgary, Alberta; Barbara Sokol, Columbus, Ohio; Margaret Sollars, Regina, Saskatchewan; Marcia M. D. Spencer, Northern Illinois; Brian C. Sproule, New South Wales, Australia; Margaret Sproule, New South Wales, Australia; John Stanford, New South Wales, Australia; Winifred Stanford, New South Wales, Australia; Sarah W. Staton, Palm Beach, Florida; Eileen Stewart, Northampton, England; Gillian Stewart, Northampton, England; Jane Stewart, Houston, Texas; Joel Stewart, Houston, Texas; John Stewart, Northampton, England.

John P. Thornton, Edmonton, Alberta; Frank Thorpy, Auckland, New Zealand; Holly Towers, London; Leopold S. Tuchman, Hollywood, California.

Pamela Vandyke Price, London; Ross T. Vernon, Windsor, Ohio; May Vivian-Cooper, Australia.

Robert C. Ward, Miami, Florida; Richard S. Webster, Northern Illinois; Ian S. Wickenden, Surrey Hills, England; Katharine Wiersum, Surrey, England; Richard Wiersum, Surrey, England; Julius Wile, New York; Audrey Wilkerson, Cotswolds, England; Ian J. Witter, New South Wales, Australia; Jack A. Witter, New South Wales, Australia; Theda A. Witter, New South Wales, Australia; Benson Wolman, Columbus, Ohio; Jerilyn Wolman, Columbus, Ohio; Gail Wright, London.

Harry Yoxall, London; Muktar Yusuf, London.

Mel Zuckerman, New York.

Aperitif

This book *is* a celebration.

The International Wine & Food Society is fifty years old, and proud of it. Our *Menu Book* is a collection of recipes – gathered all over the world – for practical use by anyone, anywhere who enjoys imaginative cooking.

The Society is made up of men and women who think it's natural to prepare good ingredients lovingly, to choose wine with care, and to serve both with style. In that sense, they believe that every meal is – or could be – a celebration.

André Louis Simon, the founder, told the first members in 1933 that "dull meals never did anyone any good", and he travelled the world proclaiming this gospel. He acquired so many disciples that by the time André left us (aged 93 – he was a good advertisement for his own philosophy), there were members of nearly forty nationalities and local groups from Scandinavia to New Zealand. There were also innumerable imitators.

We ourselves are both life members of the Society. We meet hundreds of our fellows wherever we travel, and the gastronomic gossip is always exciting. This book goes a stage further. We asked the branches in every country to send us tested recipes and ideas, added some of our own, and made a book.

We've set it up as a series of menus – six lunches, nine dinners-with-suppers, a breakfast, a picnic, and three more occasions, plus two subsequent sections of assorted recipes and some basic broths, pastries, and a vinaigrette – with coffee to follow.

Each menu is preceded by several discursive culinary and vinous paragraphs signed, respectively, AWS and HD-M, and the drinks, like the recipes, roam the world. Wherever possible, we've tried to incorporate contributors' suggestions for wines with food, but since many interesting wines are unavailable and even unheard-of world-wide, Hugo has come up with hand after hand of playing possibilities, ranging from fine red burgundy to chocolate-flavoured Wagga Wagga. The thought has not been to praise Great Bottles or to arrange rigid marriages, but to prize wine as a condiment whose alliance with food gives much to the enjoyment of both.

Each chapter of menus has been disposed in a vaguely seasonal way – at least north of the Equator – from late winter/spring back to hard frosts, and there are indications for procedure – "order of battle" for preparing and eating the meal – outlined in each set of culinary paragraphs.

So what's it all about, this Wine & Food Society cooking, fifty years on? Not *haute*, not *nouvelle*, just *bonne*, with a good eye to all sorts of compelling ingredients like the renascent American caviar, haggis and hare, wild mushrooms – once ignored, now desired – exotic leaves and edible flowers, and the continuing tradition, strong since the Society's origins, of interest in the food of all sorts of cultures.

We were sent scores of recipes, and our choice has leaned towards the ethnic, the regional, the unusual, and the simple. Some of the best came from members who said they weren't really cooks – so maybe the rest of us try too hard. The recipes we liked least – and so have not printed – were either ostentatious "party pieces" or involved the unnecessary torture of good ingredients. Others not included are those which resembled each other too closely, could not be adapted for world-wide use, or too nearly echoed already-published material.

Needless to say, the selection of dishes is highly personal; another partnership would have chosen differently. Our own recipes, with which this volume is heavily truffled, give you a notion of some of our preferences. And throughout the book we've assumed that good bread will usually be on the table, that cheese will often precede the dessert, and that condiments include a jug or bottle of cool water.

We ask the indulgence of contributors whose recipes have – on our own initiative or the advice of testers – been somehow altered. We can assure them that the change has always been for good reasons. And how we've been helped by all those testers! Each dish has been tried out, often several times and even in various countries, so as – we hope – to get things right for everyone. (But if some ingredient is lacking where you live or have settled, a lively imagination should suggest its substitute). No testers have been more zealous than the members of the

Northern Illinois Wine & Food Society who fought through "blinding snow, ice, and high winds" to a "Testing-Tasting" that resulted in a number of excellent ideas.

A list of all testers, members, and others who sent recipes is on pages xi to xiv. They range from all the (living) former Society Chairmen to a high number of epicurean doctors and to restaurateurs like John Bruno, Guy Mouilleron, and Michel Bourdin. We have gastronomic writers like Pamela Vandyke Price and Colman Andrews, wine experts such as Harry Yoxall, Julius Wile, Len Evans and Harriet Lembeck, and the blessing of cookery mentors Lesley Faull and Lyn Hall and their excellent schools. If anyone who should be listed has been omitted, please forgive us.

In addition, many friends – not all of them Society members – have taken an interest in this book and given us important technical help. Particularly, we thank Kathleen O'Mahoney, a talented cook of Johannesburg; Elizabeth and William Kivlan, whose knowledge of regional foods stretches from Georgia to Provence; the Comte de Lur Saluces (could one have a better adviser on the marriage of fine food to the wines of Sauternes?); Max and Joy Lake of Pokolbin in New South Wales, who, amid other talents, are wonderful cooks and hosts; Lesley Faull's daughter Alicia Wilkinson, who answered many questions on South African ingredients; and chefs Giuliano and Miro Pertusini who taught us not to be fearful of wild mushrooms. We are especially grateful for the good counsel of Arthur Crockett, butcher in the parish of St Marylebone, London.

Above all, we thank the members of the Society's Council for their confidence; Lord Swaythling and John Cleese for buoying our spirits with amusing letters of encouragement; Judith Elliott, Louise Bloomfield and Hilary Duguid of Heinemann for their patience; and not least each other for keeping our tempers – well, most of the time.

Please read the "note to cooks" about to follow. It contains vital clues to making head and tail of this book of recipes planned for use the world over.

A note to cooks

or

If we were using this book, some things we would want to know first

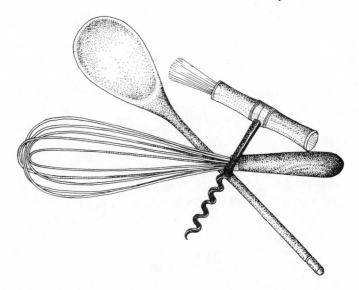

Compiling a volume of international recipes for world-wide consumption is a perilous challenge: one cook's flour, cream, and sugar are not like another's, what's "grilled" by the British is "broiled" in America, and as for cups, grams, and deci-centi-millilitres, please don't mention them!

But before the particularities, here are a few general comments. We assume that, as far as possible, all ingredients – vegetables, herbs, fish, meat, poultry, and lemon juice – will be fresh except where noted, and of the finest available quality; that olive oil, when specified, is the best you can find and that this will be farm-produced, low-acid first-pressing; that salt is "sea" or "rock" and pepper the aromatic black – not white – in the form of peppercorns, and that both will be ground for use as needed. We hope your vanilla, when not the bean, will be the "extract" – prepared by macerating beans in an alcohol solution – and never the cheap and bogus "flavouring".

An egg we reckon as weighing about 60 grams/2 ounces, except where noted, and all eggs should be used at room temperature. By raisins we mean seeded or seedless, and spoonfuls will be level unless indicated. All ovens are assumed to be pre-heated, hot things to be served on hot plates, and we are greatly in favour of carving meat in the kitchen and reheating it – as explained in the text – rather than carving at table with the risk of cold platefuls. There are several recipes for "hand-made" sorbets; if you use an ice cream machine, proceed instead as the manufacturer tells you.

Since out-of-season, imported tomatoes tend to look uniform and sensational and taste of nothing – at least in northern Europe – we sometimes suggest canned plum tomatoes, picked in their prime for maximum flavour. This is not to say we're rabid seasonalists; we love the luxury of happening on good crayfish, scallops, melon, mushrooms, or peppers that have flown or driven in from somewhere, and you'll see that here and there we recommend them.

As you gather, we have strong prejudices, and you'll notice we favour garlic, fresh ginger root, tomatoes, sweet peppers, saffron, sorrel, mint, and – yes! – cream; that we value champagne-method wine as part of the cooking, and that rice appears frequently.

You'll probably detect a lack of enthusiasm for freezing. Interestingly, few of our contributors referred to the technique, and while we think it has suitable and sometimes vital uses, as a catch-all it's too often abused. If terrines or pâtés are frozen, for instance, their texture grows soggy and any garlic strong and nasty. But the food processor (like the blender and hand-held electric beater) we find indispensable, and where we recommend its use, the steel blade is understood to be in place unless another one is prescribed.

So many people now have a stack of basic cookbooks that we've excluded description of techniques like boiling eggs, cooking rice, making mayonnaise, boning a chicken leg, and sterilising jam jars, since these procedures have so often been given. But let's take the plunge and tackle those ingredients.

Wheat flour

North American all-purpose flour is stronger than British plain flour
which is similar to French flour and we're told is more or less equivalent
to Australian plain and to South African cake flour! But for the recipes
here, *plain flour* will be the term used to designate any of the above.

Butter

The American terms "sweet" and "fresh" will be covered by the word
unsalted, and when *butter* alone is indicated, we mean the salted or
slightly-salted first-grade product. Margarine never.

Cream

A complex subject which we will drastically simplify by using *thick
cream* to designate fresh cream of at least 30% butterfat which can be
whipped and does not curdle when boiled. This will cover the notions
of double cream, and of whipping cream whether "light" or "heavy" –
but *not* the Australian "thickened" cream, which includes gelatine and
is not recommended. If *cream* alone is specified, use any of the above, or
an alternative of about 20% butterfat which may be known to you as
"single" or "coffee" cream. *Sour cream* will mean the commercially-
cultured product of 18–20% butterfat which curdles if boiled.

Sugar

British, Australian, South African, and New Zealand "granulated"
sugar is coarser than what is called "granulated" in the USA and is not
well-suited to smooth blending with butter in cakes and pastry. So
where Americans would use granulated or the finer grind called
"superfine" or "berry" sugar and British or Commonwealth cooks
"castor" sugar, we have written:

   X grams/ounces/cups castor (granulated) sugar.

Granulated in this instance applies only to Americans. If we write
granulated without alternative, it applies to everyone, as in certain
contexts the variations in grind don't matter. Any granulated sugar can
of course be ground finer in a blender.

   The finest grind of all will be designated *icing* for British and
Commonwealth readers and *confectioners'* for Americans.

   Where *brown sugar* is called for, we mean soft and light, not dark,
unless specified.

Gelatine or gelatin

By this we mean the unflavoured variety, and will measure it by weight and spoon if powdered – rather than by envelope, as contents of envelopes vary – and by numbers of "leaves" as an alternative for European cooks. But we know that blanket translations can present problems when applied to gelatine, so if you think a specific quantity wrong in your context, please adjust it.

And following on with the notion of translation, throughout the text we have freely mixed languages among recipe titles and usually provided the meaning in English – or at least explained it. Our spellings are British and the following definitions are useful to remember:

aubergine is an egg-plant

bacon: a "rasher" equals a slice, and "streaky" equals belly

baking sheet means a cookie sheet

biscuit: British = crisp, unleavened cake (either sweet or salty) like a "snap" or an American "cookie" or "cracker"; American = soft, small cake like a scone or muffin.

bread: whole meal equals whole wheat, more or less

cornflour equals cornstarch

courgettes mean zucchini

gherkins are small pickled cucumbers called *cornichons* in French

grilling equals broiling

kitchen paper means absorbent paper towels sold by the roll

peppers: sweet green and red peppers, the broad members of the capsicum family, are what's popularly known as "bell" peppers in the USA

sauté pan means frying-pan or (USA) skillet

sultanas equal white or yellow raisins

In all cases where an ingredient is in brackets, this indicates the American equivalent.

And finally, the question of weights and measures. We give them in metric and avoirdupois equivalents and where appropriate, by volume. But to our American readers we cannot stress enough the desirability of measuring dry and solid ingredients by weight. Alice speaks as an American converted first to ounces and pounds of, for example, flour or onions, and then to the same in grams and kilos!

Use of a scale streamlines the art of cooking and gives you a much truer sense of ingredients in proportion to one another, and familiarity with the metric system enables you to "read" a culinary language which is, at least in theory, international. So, although we give flour and sugar in US cups and small measurements of dry ingredients in tablespoons –

as well as sometimes grams and ounces – we have not, in the interests of worthwhile progress, done so with everything.

After much thought, consultation with fellow cooks in several countries and with the Weights and Measures Authority, plus examination of what's marked on measuring spoons and vessels in a number of popular stores for kitchen supplies, we've chosen millilitres as the most universally acceptable metric unit of liquid measure. Quantities will be shown first in millilitres or litres, followed by Imperial and then, where appropriate, American measuring units.

As far as possible, equivalents are given in round figures, so that although the Imperial fluid ounce is smaller than the American – making the Imperial litre 35 fluid ounces instead of the American 32 – we've tended to overlook this difference and call a fluid ounce the quantity equal to 30 millilitres, and a tablespoon a tablespoon (15 millilitres), regardless of country. Equally, 1 ounce avoirdupois will be treated as 30 grams, although the true equivalent everywhere is 28.35. Hence, a pound will be 30 × 16 = 480 grams, rather than 453.6. Provided everything else is in proportion, these discrepancies do not matter, except in the case of "cups" of flours and of various sugars, whose measurements we've adjusted to suitable contexts.

And sometimes, quantities are not specified but suggested by a "pinch" of salt – the amount you can pick up between thumb and two forefingers – or a "dash" of brandy and a "knob" of butter, because part of the essence of good cooking is not measurement but an educated instinct for combination.

When we speak of *pints* and *litres* in these recipes, we mean the Imperial measures of 20 and 35 fluid ounces (600 and 1000 millilitres) respectively; whereas *cups* and *quarts* will designate American measures of 8 and 32 fluid ounces only.

Oven temperatures are given first in Celsius (round figures), then in Fahrenheit, finally in British gas oven settings, as in "gas mark 5".

At long last, after ten lines of abbreviations, *bon appétit!*

millilitres: ml
centimetres: cm
inches: in
grams: g
kilograms: kg
ounces: oz
fluid ounces: fl oz
pounds: lb
teaspoons: teasp
tablespoons: tbs

Lunch and Luncheons

Luncheon with the French

for six

ÉCREVISSES À LA CRÈME
Crayfish in cream

GIGOT AU BEAUJOLAIS
Leg of lamb braised in beaujolais

GRATIN DAUPHINOIS
Gratin of potatoes

SALADE DE CRESSON
Watercress salad

PLÂTEAU DE FROMAGES
A selection of cheeses

LES GELÉES DE ST-CLÉMENT
St Clement's jellies

Luncheon with the French
for six

Harry W. Yoxall, to whom this book is dedicated, is the doyen and former President of the Wine & Food Society, former Chairman of Condé Nast Publications, a prolific writer, and the only Englishman to win the Prix Littéraire of the Confrérie des Chevaliers du Tastevin, for his book *The Wines of Burgundy*. So it's appropriate that this luncheon be built round some dishes and wines served to him at the Lyon home of "a Burgundian gastronome of fierce local patriotism".

Harry's pleasure in French cooking is not life-long. In 1903, at the age of seven, he was taken to Normandy and thought the food "disgusting". Whoever heard of prunes with pork, of vinegar in sauces, breakfasts of rolls with hot chocolate, and the complete lack of porridge and marmalade? He took comfort in peaches and nectarines, costing one sou apiece.

Yet, by the mid 1970s, Harry's tastes had developed, and *écrevisses à la crème*, prepared by the Lyonnais' daughter, were decidedly welcome. We mean here the true freshwater crayfish of about 10 cm/4 in length, not the *langouste* or spiny lobster. The meal was on a Lenten Friday and the family Roman Catholic, so meat, in fact, was absent. We've added a leg of lamb braised in the regional wine, the braising liquid then turned into sauce. With this, a classic *gratin dauphinois* – potatoes baked and browned in cream and milk – our recipe that of the Lyonnais' wife.

To follow, "watercress served alone, to refresh the mouth", as expressed by Taillevent, Charles VI's fourteenth-century chef. Then cheese, well-selected and perfectly ripe; Harry might have tasted a Mont d'Or, rigotte de Condrieu, or a St-Marcellin, all soft varieties

4

from the Lyonnais region. But Hugo thinks nothing partners mature wine better than a firm, nutty cheese like an English Cheddar or a French Cantal. So choose your style.

And for dessert to end this rich and traditional meal, a cooling pair of "jellies" – orange and lemon – in the English sense of clear, sweetened fruit-juice bound with gelatine, the name a French fantasy on the children's ditty, "Oranges and lemons say the bells of St Clement's".

Of course, the occasion need not be Lenten, but at any moment when live crayfish and young or youngish (but not baby) lamb should coincide. Southern hemisphere take note! In many places, crayfish, like scallops, have become non-seasonal, either through farming or air freight; as I write, live crustaceans flown from Turkey are on sale at the fishmonger.

The *écrevisses* and lamb need last-minute attention, the *gratin* can be kept hot for half an hour once baked, the salad is two minutes' work when you're ready to eat it. The cheeses should be waiting at room temperature, and the jellies are made a day in advance, then chopped and assembled before the meal.   AWS

Harry's Burgundian friend "was not only a great wine-lover, but bought in the barrel, with expert knowledge, direct from the *vignerons*, skilfully bottled the wines himself, and let them rest for years in his cool, dark cellar . . . We had a Bâtard-Montrachet with the *écrevisses*". Hardly any of us bottle our own burgundy, but this sumptuous recipe deserves one of the best whites you have – a chardonnay from a good California producer, a fine *spätlëse* hock (not calling itself *trocken*) or Rhine riesling, a round but not woody white rioja from Spain, or one of the remarkable steens which the South Africans have begun to export.

Cooking wine should never be just any-old. We braised the lamb in Morgon '78, a beaujolais provided for the purpose by Anthony Berry, whose family firm of vintners, Berry Bros & Rudd of London, is nearing completion of its third century. There was enough left for Alice and me to have a glass each with the meat; HWY and his friends had gone one better with the *gratin dauphinois* and drunk a Bonnes-Mares from the Côtes de Nuits. Undoubtedly both dishes call for something rich and full; if you started with a white rioja, it might be fun now to try the red, preferably a *gran reserva*, or one of the robust cabernet sauvignons from the Australian Hunter Valley.

As Harry continues, "The great bottle, or magnum rather, the Grands-Echézeaux '47, came with the cheese. The dinner was in the mid-seventies, and the wine had rested in one place for twenty-five years. '45 and '49 are more famous vintages, but I've never known anything more satisfying than this '47 – majestic but silken, the very perfection of balance". Take your cue from the Lyonnais, and give this well-considered food the accolade it merits. If Italian wines are more accessible than French, perhaps a Brunello di Montalcino from Tuscany; if you are not in Europe, a fine bottle based on the pinot noir or shiraz grape will justly partner the cheese.

Harry doesn't say so, but it seems reasonable to assume this meal would have ended with a *petit digestif* of brandy, or *prunelle* – the sloe liqueur of Burgundy. We suggest you follow either lead, but in any case the jellies – unaccompanied by wine – will make a welcome pause for breath.

HD-M

Écrevisses à la crème

40 live crayfish
60 g/2 oz butter
Salt
Cognac or other brandy
9 shallots

Three 15-ml spoons/3 tbs
    finely-chopped parsley
Concentrated tomato paste
270 ml/9 fl oz/1 copious cup thick
    cream
Pepper

Wash and drain the crayfish, remove the black intestine of each by twisting and pulling out the middle tail fin – a process neither you nor they will enjoy.

Melt the butter in a very large sauté pan – or two of medium size – turn the heat up and sauté the crayfish for 5 minutes, tossing; the high heat will kill them quickly.

Add a little salt, about 30 ml/2 tbs cognac or other brandy, and flame this, shaking the pan till the fire dies. Mince the shallots and add them, with the parsley, plus a little tomato paste for colour. Cover the pan and cook the crustaceans over a low heat for another 5–7 minutes; taste one to see if they are done.

Remove the fish with a slotted spoon, take out any that have turned black, and keep the others hot on a large platter in a low oven. Add cream to the sauce, reduce it to a slightly thickened consistency and good flavour, add a little more cognac or brandy to taste, pepper, and salt if necessary.

Mound the crayfish on their platter, pour over the sauce, and serve with finger bowls of iced water at each place, plus extra plates for discarded shells.

Harry W. Yoxall, London, England

Gigot au beaujolais

A 2½ kg/5 lb leg of lamb
2 cloves garlic
A small piece of fresh ginger root
A large onion
2 carrots
60 g/2 oz butter
A little oil

2 sprigs fresh tarragon, or a pinch
    of dried if fresh is unobtainable
480 ml/16 fl oz/2 cups fruity red
    wine such as a young beaujolais,
    or any gamay or syrah (shiraz)
    wine
Salt and pepper
One 5-ml spoon/1 teasp arrowroot

Wipe the lamb and trim away its excess fat. Peel and sliver the garlic; pierce the meat with incisions, especially near the bone, and slide in the slivers. Peel the ginger and rub it all over the surfaces of the leg.

Peel and slice the onion and carrots, melt half the butter in a deep, heavy oval cocotte or casserole just big enough to take the lamb, add a drop of oil, and brown the meat quickly on all sides. Remove the lamb, clean the casserole, add remaining butter, and sweat the vegetables over a low heat until they begin to soften; turn the heat high to colour them slightly. If the butter then burns, pour it away. Add tarragon, pour in the wine, toss in some salt, and bring the liquid to a simmer. Slide in the meat, return wine to the simmer, cover the casserole – lid slightly ajar – and braise the meat in a 180°C/350°F/gas mark 4 oven for about 1 hour and 15 minutes, basting occasionally. It should emerge pink.

Take the lamb from its casserole and let it rest in a warm place for 20 minutes. Meanwhile, strain the braising liquid, pressing on the vegetables, remove most of its fat, and boil briskly to reduce by about a third. Cool slightly.

Dissolve the arrowroot in a little water, whisk this into the wine and let it simmer until the sauce barely thickens. Correct seasoning.

Carve the lamb onto a hot platter, spoon over a little sauce and serve the rest in a warm boat.

Gratin dauphinois

1¼ kg/2½ lb waxy potatoes, large if
  possible
Butter
Salt, pepper, and grated nutmeg

150 ml/5 fl oz/scant ⅔ cup each of
  thick cream and milk

Butter a shallow oval baking dish – earthenware is good – of 30–35 cm/12–14 in length.

Peel and slice the potatoes – the easiest way is on a mandoline – about ½ cm/⅛ in thick; don't wash the slices but dry them in cloths. Arrange slices in layers of overlapping rows along the dish, salting and peppering each layer, with just a little nutmeg here and there. When the dish is full to about 1½ cm/½ in from the top, dot on some butter, mix the cream and milk and pour them slowly just to cover the potatoes.

Bake this in a 155°C/310°F/gas mark 2 oven for 1–1½ hours or until the potatoes are tender and brown and the milk absorbed. Or, if baking with the lamb in a 180°C/350°F/gas mark 4 oven, put the gratin beneath the meat and cook the two for about 1¼ hours.

The gratin can be held, covered in foil, in a *bain-marie* (pan of shallow water kept just below the simmer) atop the stove while the lamb is allowed to rest and then carved.

Serve the gratin hot in its dish.

Harry W. Yoxall

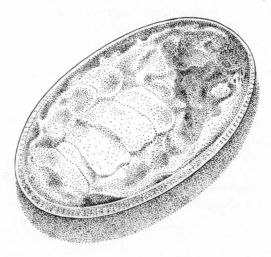

Les gelées de St-Clément

Orange jelly
4–5 large oranges
About 30 ml/2 tbs strained lemon
    juice
240 ml/8 fl oz/1 cup water

15g/½ oz powdered gelatine or 4
    leaves European gelatine
90 g/3 oz/scant ½ cup granulated
    sugar

Lemon jelly
4–5 lemons
300 ml/½ pint/1¼ cups water
20 g/a generous ½ oz powdered
    gelatine or 4½ leaves European
    gelatine

180 g/6oz/ very generous ¾ cup
    granulated sugar

Sprigs of mint or orange blossom as garnish

To make the orange jelly, pare the zest (without pith) of 2 oranges, squeeze and strain enough juice from all the oranges to give you 300 ml/½ pint/1¼ cups. Add the lemon juice.

In a medium saucepan, soften the powdered gelatine in a little of the water. When the gelatine has swelled, add remaining water and swirling, dissolve the powder over a low heat. If using leaf gelatine, soak it in the full amount of water, and when soft, dissolve as above.

Add the orange juice, zest, and sugar. Heat to just below the boiling point, remove pan from the fire, cover, and steep the zest in the liquid for 20 minutes. Strain into a bowl through a sieve lined with muslin or cheesecloth, discard the zest, cool the jelly, and refrigerate overnight.

Make the lemon jelly exactly as above, using 240 ml/8 fl oz/1 cup of strained lemon juice to 300 ml/½ pint/1¼ cups of water, and steeping the pared zest of 2 lemons for the same amount of time. Strain into a second bowl, cool and refrigerate overnight.

To serve the jellies, unmould by dipping both bowls into a basin of hot water. Turn out each jelly onto a garlic-free board, use a large knife to chop them separately – not too fine, or you'll lose the sparkle – and pile 2 half-moons of jelly, one of each colour, to face one another on 6 dessert plates. Garnish the centre of each join with a sprig of fresh mint, or some orange blossom if the season is right and your fresh oranges were imported! The moons can be assembled just before the meal, refrigerated, and garnished as you serve them.

Fish bowl
for six

SALADE D'ASPERGES, SAUCE SPÉCIALE
Asparagus with a piquant mayonnaise

FISH BOWL

THE MAD PANCAKE

Fish bowl
for six

A lunch in the spring or early summer – the asparagus season – and an informal one, perhaps outside; a meal for eating with the fingers and for mopping up soup with good bread.

Michel Bourdin, chef of London's Connaught Hotel, does not belong to the Society but is a friend and favourite of many members, all devotees of the classic French and English dishes that flow from his well-drilled kitchen. The *sauce spéciale* for cooled asparagus was invented while Michel was *sous-chef* at Maxim's in Paris and is simple and elegant. A variation, for saucing mussels, is given at the end of the recipe.

The fish bowl, from Californian food and wine writer Colman Andrews, is spiced and filled with surprises in the best tradition of maritime soups. The sharpness of sorrel or other pungent greens makes it that much more interesting. The fish is cooked unboned, so beware of this when eating.

Our pancake is crazy, "mad" in the British sense, rising all over the place and quite uncontrolled. The recipe is for six, but Hugo has been seen to down five portions at a sitting!

All the elements in this menu can be prepared early: asparagus bundled, sauce finished, soup partly cooked, pancake batter ready, but the final launch of each dish is straightforward and happens at the last minute.

AWS

The big decision here is what to drink with the fish. A fruity white burgundy or, better, an Hermitage from the Rhône or some chardonnay from Victoria, Australia would be highly acceptable. Colman Andrews recommends a "tart, acidic white – muscadet or gros plant", but adds that his own preference would be for "a fruity minor red – beaujolais or côtes du rhône, *nouveau* or otherwise, or a gentle red wine from the Roman hills, a Californian gamay or light zinfandel – preferably slightly chilled". Variety indeed!

The creamy mayonnaise with asparagus would kill a white burgundy or other chardonnay, so go for Colman's "minor fruity reds", or try a rosé – not the delicate Tavel, but an Italian Tyrol or robust Béarn from the French Pyrénées.

The pancake is a bit of fun, so we have made some zany matches. *Vin fou du Jura* (from eastern France), Japanese plum wine (from those wonderful people who, according to legend, gave you "Finest Scotch Whisky, made from Real English Grapes"), Austria's sparkling apricot, Danish cherry Kirsberry or an English orange wine. Maybe you can think of something wilder?

HD-M

Salade d'asperges, sauce spéciale

1400 g/3 lb green asparagus
Salt
360 ml/12 fl oz/1½ cups home-made
   mayonnaise, with two 5-ml
   spoons/2 teasp French mustard,
   preferably Dijon, added to the

yolks at the beginning, plus a
   little more to finish the sauce
180 ml/6 fl oz/¾ cup thick cream
1 heaped 15-ml spoon/1 heaped tbs
   chopped fresh chives
Salt and pepper

Cut off the first 1½–2½ cm/½–1 in of tough asparagus stems and peel each stalk. Make them up into string-tied bundles of 6–8 stalks each and boil in salted water for 5–10 minutes until tender. Put the asparagus on to kitchen paper or tea-towels, cut the strings, drain and pat them dry. Serve when just cooled with a pretty bowl of *sauce spéciale*, made in advance as follows, and well-chilled.

Sauce spéciale
Prepare the mayonnaise and whip the cream to soft peaks, fold the two together, stir in the chives, add salt and pepper and a hint more mustard if you think it necessary.

For use in the mussel season as a condiment to a salad of those freshly-steamed bivalves, make the mayonnaise with an orange-based mustard, replace the chives with tiny dice of blanched orange and lemon zest, and serve the mussels in their half-shells with a bit of sauce on each.

Michel Bourdin, London, England

Fish bowl

If you like spicy foods, be generous with the pepper flakes or chili and paprika. Otherwise go easy on these – the soup will not suffer.

Olive oil
2 medium onions
3 large cloves garlic
4 medium tomatoes, or about 480 g/1 lb canned tomatoes, including their juices
60 g/2 oz anchovy fillets, separated
1½ litres/2½ pints/6 cups fish broth (page 220)
Ground paprika
Dried red pepper flakes or a fresh chili pepper
Oregano
Salt if necessary

About 1900 g/4 lb fresh ocean fish – at least three kinds – such as halibut, bass, tuna or tunny fish, swordfish, grouper, red snapper, red mullet, brill, cod, haddock – depending on country and availability
2 good handfuls finely-shredded sorrel (stems removed) or other slightly bitter greens like Batavian endive, mustard, kale, or even watercress
Pepper
Toasted French bread, good butter

Lightly cover the bottom of a large stock-pot or saucepan with olive oil, peel and finely chop the onions and garlic and sweat them over a low heat until translucent and turning golden.

Meanwhile, peel, seed, and coarsely chop the fresh tomatoes, or chop the tinned ones and heat either in a saucepan with their juices, the anchovy fillets and 480 ml/16 fl oz/2 cups of fish broth. When heated through, purée the mixture in a blender or food processor and add it to the sweated onions, together with the remaining broth.

Season to taste with paprika, dried pepper flakes (or the seeded and minced chili pepper), about one 5-ml spoon/1 teasp oregano, and salt if you think necessary – remember the salt of the anchovies. Let the liquid simmer on a low heat for 20–30 minutes. You can prepare the soup in advance to this stage.

When ready to finish, gut and scale the fish if this has not been done, cut them into manageable pieces and add them to the base with the sorrel or other greens and freshly-ground pepper. Simmer on a low heat until the fish is just cooked, which should take no more than 6–7 minutes. Test by tasting one of the larger pieces, and correct seasoning.

Serve with plenty of lightly-toasted French bread and, for those who want it, butter.

Colman Andrews, Alta California Wine & Food Society, USA

The mad pancake

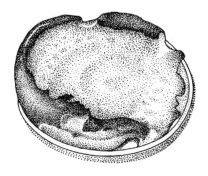

Basically a Yorkshire pudding or popover batter, slightly sweetened, with less milk and flour than either. Since some English people used to eat Yorkshire with syrup for dessert on Sundays after the roast, this is not a new concept for the British.

In a newspaper article published during the German Occupation of Paris, the writer Colette gave her recipe for *la flognarde*, a similar pancake long claimed as their own by both Burgundians and Limousins; she later said that this single paragraph had created more stir among readers than anything else she had ever written!

75 g/2½ oz/½ cup plain flour
One 15-ml spoon/1 tbs castor
  (granulated) sugar
A pinch each of salt and ground
  cinnamon
2 eggs

120 ml/4 fl oz/½ cup milk
30 g/1 oz butter
One 15-ml spoon/1 tbs icing
  (confectioners') sugar
A tart jam like apricot or
  gooseberry

Sift the flour, castor or granulated sugar, salt, and cinnamon into a bowl, make a well in the centre and break into this the 2 eggs. Gradually add the milk to the eggs, whisking in the surrounding flour, until half the liquid has been incorporated. Beat the mixture vigorously to eliminate lumps and whisk in the remaining milk. Beat till ultra-smooth, cover and let rest for an hour or more.

Twenty minutes before you want to serve the pancake, melt the butter in a quiche dish or low metal pie tin of about 26½ cm/10½ in diameter, make the container very hot, stir the batter and pour it in. Put this quickly into a 220°C/425°F/gas mark 7 oven and leave it undisturbed for 20 minutes. It will rise wildly round the edges, look like camels' humps in the middle, and be thoroughly gilded.

Remove from the oven, sieve over the icing or confectioners' sugar, and rush pancake to the table – like a soufflé, it will not wait. Carve into 6 wedges and serve with a small bowl of well-whisked jam.

A summer tricolour
for four

CHILLED AVOCADO SOUP,
MELBA TOASTS WITH HERBED EGGS

SPINACH AND SORREL SALAD

CEVICHE

BURGHUL AND MINT SALAD

SUMMER PUDDING

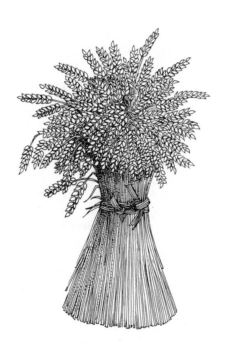

A summer tricolour
for four

A summer lunch, in shades of green, white, and a touch of red, July or
January, depending on your hemisphere, and out of doors: why not that
now-unfashionable concept, a *ladies'* lunch? Women are said to be too
occupied – or preoccupied – these days to have time for such events, but
that's nonsense; we'll never miss a chance for good food!

Pamela Vandyke Price, a *grand cru* among the world's wine writers
and a member of the Society since the days of André Simon, starts
things off with a quickly made, sophisticated avocado soup to which a
little vermouth adds an interesting nuance. Hugo and I contributed the
crunch of toasts with herbed and sesamed eggs.

The three salads should be served together, as a line of green and
white platters from which each lady helps herself. We've added the
sharp bite of raw sorrel to Brad Blakeman's spinach, and think it an
excellent companion to Peg May's *ceviche*, a Peruvian dish in which fish
is "cooked" by marination in citrus juices. The technique is akin to the
method for West Indian *escabeche*, whose fish is sautéed before
immersion in fruit juice and oil with pungent additives.

Burghul or *bulgur* is the boiled, dried, and cracked wheat used in
Middle Eastern cooking, and is the basis of many Lebanese, Turkish,
and Armenian dishes, of which the best known to Westerners is
probably *tabbouleh* from the Lebanon.

I can't think of a better finish here than the delectable and seemingly
artless summer pudding. A Wiltshire restaurant once served the two of
us a whole one from which to cut a slice each; its crimson dome had
almost collapsed by the time we stopped.

The soup, toast, herbed eggs, and basics of the spinach salad should be done on the morning of your lunch. The other salads can be mixed the previous night and assembled before you eat, while the pudding can have a two-day start.

AWS

If you are Californian or South African, you probably *will* serve this meal outside. If you are English, then I can only hope so. In or out, it would be fun to precede it with red or white "spritzers" – light wine enlivened with sparkling mineral water, served cold.

Writing this on a dull London December morning, I take heart from the thought of sunny glasses of gently chilled gamay, or rosé from Tavel on the Rhône, an Alsatian riesling or a Portuguese *vinho verde*. Nothing too grand or dramatic for the mixed pungency of sorrel, citrus and yoghurt.

But then . . .! Your best sauternes, a sweet champagne, or one of those German or Austrian *beerenauslesen* that are usually so difficult to marry with food. Cool, and sipped long and lazily between mouthfuls of the lovely amalgam of soft summer fruits. Its prospect makes the English winter bearable.

HD-M

Chilled avocado soup

Make this early in the morning of your luncheon; it should not get so cold as to dull the flavour.

1–2 large or 3–4 small ripe avocados, enough to yield 260 g/8½ oz flesh
900–1200 ml/1½–2 pints/4–5 cups chicken broth (page 219)
One 1.25-ml spoon/¼ teasp grated lemon zest

Juice of half a large lemon
60 g/2 oz chopped onion
15 ml/1 tbs or more dry white vermouth
Salt and pepper
90 ml/3 fl oz/generous ⅓ cup sour cream

Snipped fresh chives and blanched, split, and toasted almonds as garnish

Put the flesh of the avocados, 900 ml/1½ pints/4 cups of the chicken stock, the lemon zest and juice, onion, vermouth, some salt and pepper into a blender or food processor and blend until all is ultra-smooth. Add more stock if necessary to thin the mixture, and whisk in the sour cream. Check the seasoning, remembering that the soup will be served chilled, which mutes the impact of salt. Transfer to a container, cover, and refrigerate.

Present the soup in 4 individual bowls and garnish with snipped chives plus some split almonds that have been browned briefly in a 180°C/350°F/gas mark 4 oven. Hand round the following toasts.

Pamela Vandyke Price, London, England

Melba toast with herbed eggs

Buy good Melba toast, or better still, make your own by slicing firm, slightly stale bread as thin as possible. Remove crusts and cut each slice into 4 cm/1½ in strips; dry them in a 120°C/250°F/gas mark ¼ oven to a crisp, light, golden-brown.

Hard-boil 3 eggs, peel and chop them and bind with some good mayonnaise, some snipped fresh chives and chervil and a few sesame seeds that have been toasted in the same oven as the split almonds. Season with salt and pepper, mix well, and just before serving the soup, lightly butter the toasts, spread them with the herbed eggs and arrange on a plate.

Spinach and sorrel salad

300 g/10 oz young, tender, and
  healthy spinach and sorrel
  leaves, ideally ⅔ spinach to ⅓
  sorrel, or all spinach if sorrel
  can't be found
4 thin rashers of unsmoked streaky
  (belly) bacon
2 spring onions (scallions)

30 ml/2 tbs lemon juice
One 5-ml spoon/½ teasp French
  mustard, preferably Dijon
One 2.5-ml spoon/1 teasp castor
  (granulated) sugar
Liberal salt and pepper
An egg yolk
60 ml/4 tbs olive or walnut oil

Stem and wash the spinach and sorrel, dry them thoroughly – preferably in a salad spinner – and cut all but 8 perfect leaves into short ribbons. Chill the lot, wrapped carefully in tea-towels.

Cut rinds from the bacon if necessary, cut each slice across into 1 cm/⅜ in strips and sauté these until crisp. Drain them on kitchen paper. Clean and finely slice the onions or scallions.

Make a dressing by beating the egg yolk into the combined lemon juice, mustard, sugar, salt, and pepper; dribble in the oil and judge the seasoning.

Just before serving, spread the uncut leaves like daisy petals fanning from the centre of a large serving plate. Toss the ribboned greens with the bacon and onions, pour on the dressing, blend thoroughly, pile the salad onto the "daisy", and bring to the table right away.

Brad Blakeman, Northern Illinois Wine & Food Society, USA

Ceviche

Frank Thorpy of the Auckland, New Zealand Wine & Food Society suggests a similar process to this – adapted from a Tahitian recipe – for South Pacific fish.

*360 g/12 oz firm white fish fillets,
  free of bones, such as sole, sea
  bass, striped bass, red snapper,
  or even sea scallops*
1 fresh chili pepper
1 sweet green pepper
6–8 spring onions (scallions)

*Two 5-ml spoons/2 teasp coriander
  seeds*
1 large clove garlic
60 ml/4 tbs lemon juice
*90 ml/3 fl oz/a generous ⅓ cup
  each of orange and lime juice*
Salt and pepper
Crisp lettuce leaves

Cut the fish fillets, on the bias, into diagonal mouthfuls of about 1½ × 2½ cm/½ × 1 in each. If using scallops, cut into bite-size pieces. Put all the fish into a china bowl. Open and thinly slice both peppers, discarding seeds; clean, trim, and sliver the onions, crush the coriander, peel and crush the garlic and stir these into the three juices. Pour the whole thing over the fish and toss well.

Refrigerate the mixture under foil for at least 4 hours, or overnight if you like, stirring periodically. The juices turn the fish opaque.

To serve, remove the garlic, drain the fish and their trimmings of juice (which can be used for soup), grind on salt and pepper, and present the chilled salad on a platter of lettuce.

Peg May, Richmond, Illinois, USA

Burghul and mint salad

Burghul is available in three "cracks" – fine, medium, and coarse – from natural food stores and Middle Eastern groceries. The medium "crack" is best here.

180 g/6 oz medium burghul
420 ml/14 fl oz/1¾ cups chicken
  broth (page 219)
1 large clove garlic
240–270 ml/8 or 9 fl oz/1
  generous cup plain yoghurt

One 1.25-ml spoon/¼ teasp ground
  cumin
A big pinch ground ginger
20 or so small black olives
A large bunch of very fresh mint
Salt and pepper
Crisp lettuce leaves

Combine the *burghul* and chicken broth in a heavy saucepan, add the peeled, chopped garlic, and bring the stock to the boil, stirring. Cover the saucepan and simmer the mixture over a very low heat for 3–5 minutes or until the stock has been absorbed.

Transfer the *burghul* to a bowl, stir in enough yoghurt to moisten the grain well without excess, add the cumin and ginger. Cool if necessary. Split the flesh of each olive, remove the stone, slice olives into strips and add these to the *burghul*. Wash, dry, and shred some mint leaves, adding these to taste – there should be quite a lot of mint – and leaving plenty of leaves intact for garnish. Add salt and pepper to taste and judge whether to increase the cumin and ginger – they should not predominate.

Let the salad stand, covered, in a cool place until needed – it can be made the night before if you like. To serve, arrange some lettuce on a plate and mound the *burghul* in an oval atop it, smoothing with wet hands to mould the grain into an attractive shape. Garnish smartly with a row of mint leaves laid diagonally along the centre, fill a bowl with lettuce leaves and encourage the guests to roll a little salad into a leaf and eat each roll in two bites.

Summer pudding

Why should the British, blessed with black, red, and white currants that coincide with raspberries, be the only nation to enjoy one of the world's best desserts? Americans, along with others who don't grow or can't find fresh currants, can substitute blueberries and cherries, or logan and blackberries if these have appeared on the cane.

In the absence of currants, lemon juice must be added to the berries' juices for a tart result. All the fruit, need we say, should be fresh.

A large, square loaf of slightly stale, unsliced white bread
240 g/8 oz black currants or loganberries
240 g/8 oz each raspberries and blueberries or cherries

120 g/4 oz white currants, or cherries if not used above, or blackberries
About 210 g/7 oz/1 cup granulated sugar
Lemon juice if necessary
Thick cream

Have ready a 1200 ml/2 pint/5 cup china basin for steamed puddings, as pictured, or a narrow bowl of equivalent size.

Remove crusts from the bread and slice it 1 cm/⅜ in thick. Cut a bread circle to fit the base of the bowl exactly, and 8 or so wedges of bread to line the sides and form a snug case, without gaps, to contain the fruit, as shown below.

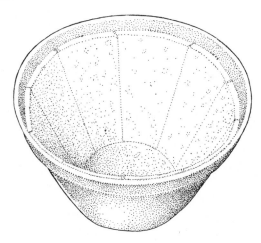

Pick over and wash the fruits, stoning and halving the cherries. If using black currants, put them with the sugar into a large heavy saucepan, and cook, covered, over a low heat for about 5 minutes; they take longer to yield their juices than the other fruits. Then add the remaining berries (or throw all the berries and sugar together, from the beginning, if black currants are not among them) and cook the mixture, covered, over a gentle heat for a further 5–7 minutes until the fruit is tender without being mushy. There should be a great deal of juice. Taste, and judge whether to add the lemon.

Using a slotted spoon, scoop half the berries, without their juices, into the bread case. Put a layer of bread on the fruit, and spoon over the remaining berries, leaving juices behind. Cover this with a layer of bread that fits within the edges of the case and slowly pour over all the juice so that the whole case is saturated, inside and out.

Cover the pudding with a saucer or small plate that can just settle, right way up, inside the basin's top rim, and pile this with the weights from a scale or with unopened cans. Let the pudding cool, and refrigerate it, on a larger plate to catch any overflow, for at least 24 hours.

The pudding can be made up to two days before eating. When ready to serve, carefully remove the weights and plate, run the blunt edge of a knife gently round the sides of the basin, and invert the pudding onto a serving dish.

Slice wedges with a sharp knife, cover them with escaping juices, and pour on a healthy dollop of thick cream.

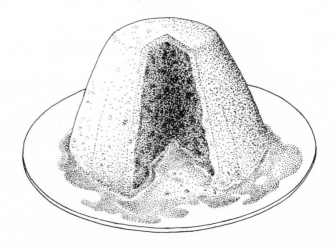

A tribute to the gardener
for six

RATATOUILLE-CAPONATA

POUSSINS EN PAPILLOTES
Young chickens in paper cases

STRAWBERRY CHARLOTTE, RED FRUITS SAUCE

A tribute to the gardener
for six

At the height of summer – late July and August, north of the equator, and a
little later than the previous meal – this is a lunch to glorify the successful
kitchen gardener. Happy the enthusiast with tomatoes, aubergines,
courgettes, sweet peppers and herbs all at the ready, with raspberries,
loganberries, and remontant or everbearing strawberries in equal
abundance – or earlier strawberries stocking the freezer. Still happier the
gardener for whom all this is cooked while he or she vegetates.

Those of us without a single quarter-acre can revel in the buying of
handsome ingredients for Mark Coventry's *ratatouille-caponata; ratatouille* a familiar Mediterranean French dish, and *caponata*, from Sicily,
contributing elements like sugar, vinegar and black olives to the tumult
of pepper and aubergine.

Lyn Hall is the founder and inspiration of La Petite Cuisine, a
wonderful cooking school near London – one of the few worth the price
of tuition – and her tiny chickens baked with herbs and vegetables in
paper cases have all the advantages of *papillote* cooking: the retention of
moisture, the great burst of aromas as papers open, the fun of eating
from your own surprise package. *Poussins* were once a strictly springtime
chicken, but in many places they are now raised commercially and like
quail are available all the year round. In the United States, where the
poussin is rare, substitute Rock Cornish hens – or squabs if you can get
these elusive birds.

The charlotte is a rosy Bavarian cream in a chemise of sponge cake.
The strawberry and chocolate tart on page 216 is a possible substitute,
but suitable only for fresh berries.

Everything here is best prepared a day ahead – the *ratatouille* and

26

poussins simply put into the oven to bake before serving. So the cook, too, can relax with the gardener!

AWS

Ratatouille and *poussins* can take almost any wine that is neither extremely delicate nor too sweet. So you may like the idea of some simple wines that evoke the garden. From the Loire, appropriately "the garden of France", a generous white anjou, or from Germany, the flowery bouquet of a badenwein.

All the *cépages* of Corsica have some scent of that island's flowering, shrubby undergrowth which Corsicans call the *maquis* – the name adopted in World War II by the French Resistance – and their wines are as redolant of this as the *poussins'* flesh after baking with lemon and fresh herbs.

Vignerons are usually too busy keeping the weeds and pests at bay to worry much how a vineyard *looks* – a matter of great concern, however, among the grape-vines of Mount Fujiyama, where Japanese gardening finds full expression. If you've come home with a bottle of the rare and exceptional Vin Noble (Suntory's answer to sauternes), now might be the time to bring it out as a partner for the charlotte. But since this is the most costly dessert wine in the world (even Yquem is cheap by comparison) you'll probably prefer to open something else! Any good-quality sweet wine would be fine, and Château St-Jean's Late Harvest Riesling from Sonoma, California, is simply ideal.

HD-M

Ratatouille-caponata

We've set down this recipe in the breezy style of the sender, who calls it a "kitchen gardener's delight, as most if not all of the ingredients ripen at about the same time. One of the beauties of the dish is that the cook can use his or her imagination, and whatever is freely available, without sticking to a rigid recipe". Hence the informality. Mark Coventry gives no quantities; we've put in a few.

The sauce is rich and piquant, and the result successful as a hot vegetable or, as here, a cool first course.

About 720 g/1½ lb each aubergines
  (egg-plants), onion, and
  courgettes (zucchini)
3 or 4 sweet red peppers
Stalks of Swiss chard – say
  240 g/8 oz
3–5 large tomatoes
Salt
Olive oil

Wine vinegar
Sugar
Fresh tarragon, basil, thyme or
  oregano, or some combination of
  these
3–4 large cloves garlic
Pepper
Pine nuts
Black olives

Peel and cube the aubergines, salt the cubes well and put them into a colander for an hour to drain away their excess moisture. Peel and finely slice the onions, cut the courgettes into chunks, the seeded peppers into thin strips, and the chard into oblique matchsticks. Peel and seed the tomatoes.

When all this is ready, separately stir-fry each vegetable (except tomatoes) with a little olive oil in a large frying pan. Drain and dry the aubergine cubes before doing so, and sauté all but the aubergine (which should be fully cooked) until no more than three-quarters done. Add more oil as necessary.

When the five vegetables are ready, pour excess oil from the empty pan, put in the tomatoes and simmer slowly for 20 minutes, breaking them up as they bubble. This is the basis for sauce; when it's well reduced, add vinegar and sugar in equal proportions for a sweet-sour effect, toss in salt to taste and whatever herbs you like, going easy on the oregano. Then add at least 3 finely-chopped cloves of garlic and simmer for 10 minutes. Taste carefully; the sauce's flavour will predominate.

Add plenty of pepper, all the previously cooked vegetables, pine nuts and black olives, give everything a good stir, and simmer briefly. Check the seasoning and transfer the *ratatouille* to a large casserole. Bake it covered in a 180°C/350°F/gas mark 4 oven for about half an hour to finish the cooking. Remove the lid for the last 5 minutes to dissipate steam.

Serve this about an hour or two from the oven.

If you like, prepare the whole thing the day before, refrigerate it and leave the half hour's baking till the morning of your luncheon. The flavours benefit.

Dr. Mark S. Coventry, Rochester, Minnesota Wine & Food Society, USA

Poussins en papillotes

6 fresh, young, oven-ready chickens, called poussins, 5–6 weeks old, weighing about 480–600 g/1–1¼ lb each, or

Rock Cornish hens (USA) of the same weight, or the young fattened pigeons called squabs

Cavity stuffing
One 120 g/4 oz onion
60 g/2 oz butter
105 g/3½ oz sausage meat
60 g/2 oz rindless lean bacon, chorizo or mortadella sausage, or German smoked pork

Five 15-ml spoons/5 tbs chopped fresh herbs like parsley and thyme
3 eggs
Fresh white breadcrumbs
Salt and pepper

Breast stuffing
120 g/4 oz butter, softened
Zest of a lemon
60 g/2 oz chorizo sausage

Six 15-ml spoons/6 tbs chopped fresh herbs, as above
Salt and pepper
12 tiny slivers of garlic

To finish
About 90 g/3 oz each peeled and trimmed carrots, celery, onion – and fennel, if available

Butter

Have the six birds to hand.

To make the cavity stuffing, peel and finely chop the onion; soften it in butter for 5 minutes over a low heat. Add the sausage meat and cook until its pinkness disappears. Remove from the heat and cool slightly. Finely chop the bacon, sausage, or smoked pork and add it with the herbs to the stuffing. Add 3 beaten eggs and enough breadcrumbs to bind.

To make the breast stuffing, beat the softened butter, grate the lemon zest, finely chop the chorizo and fresh herbs, add these to the butter, beat it to a smooth paste and season well. Divide into 6 portions, adding 2 small splinters of garlic to each.

Wipe the birds clean, season them inside, divide the first stuffing among the 6 cavities and tie together each pair of legs, thereby closing the *poussin's* vent. At the neck opening, push your fingers gently between skin and breast meat and work a portion of the lemon and herb butter into each space. Pin the neck skin back in place with a wooden toothpick, pushing toothpick well into the flesh – trouble begins if the *papillote* is punctured during handling or cooking. Tie the wings together across the back of each bird, dry, and season well.

Cut the carrots, celery, onion, and fennel into a fine *julienne* (thin strips) of about 2½ cm/1 in length and sweat this briefly in a little butter.

Liberally butter 6 large squares of greaseproof or parchment paper and season them lightly. The butter, plus the *poussin* juices, will form an aromatic sauce whose *bouquet* bursts forth as the *papillotes* open, so don't stint. Place a bird, with some julienned vegetables, into the centre of each square and close the edges of the paper with a double fold. Staple the seam at intervals of 2½ cm/1 in.

If you like, prepare the birds in their cases the previous day, refrigerate, and remove from the cold in advance of baking.

When ready, place the *papillotes* in a 205°C/400°F/ gas mark 6 oven for 40 minutes.

Have ready two plates – one hot – per guest. Present the *papillote* – to be torn open with a rush of scent – on the hot one, with the second to be used for discarding bones and paper. Have a pair of scissors handy for cutting trussing strings, and give everyone a finger bowl of iced water.

Lyn Hall, Richmond, Surrey, England

Strawberry charlotte, red fruits sauce

Sponge cake

Four 15-ml spoons/4 tbs each
    sifted plain flour and sifted
    cornflour (cornstarch)
Pinch of salt
4 eggs

Vanilla extract
60 g/4 tbs castor (granulated)
    sugar
Kirsch

Strawberry Bavarian cream

480 g/1 lb strawberries, fresh and
    ripe if possible, otherwise frozen
60 g/2 oz/scant $\frac{1}{2}$ cup icing
    (confectioners') sugar
1$\frac{1}{2}$–2 lemons
Kirsch
240 ml/8 fl oz/1 cup milk

3 egg yolks
120 g/4 oz/scant $\frac{2}{3}$ cup castor
    (granulated) sugar
15 g/$\frac{1}{2}$ oz powdered gelatine or 4
    leaves European gelatine
60 ml/4 tbs thick cream

Sauce

150 ml/5 fl oz/$\frac{2}{3}$ cup strawberry
    purée (see recipe)
240 g/8 oz each raspberries and
    loganberries, or all raspberries –
    frozen ones can be used, if
    necessary

1 lemon
1 orange
Castor or granulated sugar
Kirsch

Whole strawberries, with stems if possible, for garnish

To make the sponge cake, line a Swiss roll tin measuring about 30 ×40
cm/12 × 16 in with a sheet of buttered greaseproof or parchment paper
large enough to extend above the tin's sides.

Sift together the flours and salt. Separate the eggs, whisk vanilla into
the yolks, and beat the whites to peaks. Gradually beat in the sugar until
stiff peaks form. Whisk about a third of the whites into the yolks to
lighten them, pour this onto the remaining whites, and deftly fold the
two together, at the same time incorporating the sifted flours.

Quickly pour the batter into the lined tin, spread it evenly, tap the
tin against the work surface to settle the contents, and bake the sponge
in a 190°C/375°F/gas mark 5 oven for 15–20 minutes or until the cake is
browning and tests done. Remove the sponge – in its paper – from the
tin, let it cool, turn over and peel away the greaseproof.

Lightly butter a 1200 ml/2 pint/5 cup loaf tin measuring about $24\frac{1}{2} \times 9\frac{1}{2} \times 8$ cm/$9\frac{1}{2} \times 3\frac{3}{4} \times 3$ in. Cut the cooled sponge into 5 pieces, 1 to fit the tin's base exactly and 4 to fit the sides above, so that the strawberry cream will be completely enclosed. Lightly imbibe the cake's surfaces – those that were next to the paper – with a little kirsch mixed with water and line the tin with these.

To make the Bavarian cream, blend the strawberries (if frozen, thaw them, then drain and reserve the juices, adding a little to the subsequent purée if it seems too thick) with the icing or confectioners' sugar, the juice of $1\frac{1}{2}$ lemons, and a liberal splash of kirsch. Purée till very smooth, and taste; the result should be tart, not obviously alcoholic, and with enough sugar to give it character. Add more lemon juice and kirsch if necessary.

Make a custard by heating the milk while beating the yolks and castor or granulated sugar to form a ribbon. Set the gelatine to soak in water. Pour the milk onto the yolks, whisking vigorously; sieve this back to the milk's saucepan and bring just to the boil, whisking constantly. The custard will thicken suddenly. Immediately sieve into a chilled bowl and beat to cool the custard slightly. Melt the gelatine by swirling it over a low heat with a very little of its soaking water, sieve this into the base, add 450 ml/15 fl oz/a scant 2 cups of the strawberry purée, and mix.

Half-whip the cream, have the kirsch to hand and set the strawberry custard into a bowl of ice and water. With a rubber spatula, stir the custard to cool and thicken to the same consistency as the half-whipped cream, which brings it close to the setting point. Remove the bowl from the ice and immediately fold in the cream. Taste, and add enough kirsch – perhaps as much as 15 ml/1 tbs – to give "point" to the flavour without being obvious.

Pour this into the lined mould and let it set in the refrigerator for several hours and preferably overnight.

Make a sauce by blending the leftover strawberry purée, which equals about 150 ml/$\frac{1}{4}$ pint/$\frac{2}{3}$ cup, with the raspberries – and loganberries if used (any frozen fruit should be drained of their juices, which can be added to thin the sauce) – the juice of lemon and orange, plus sugar and kirsch to taste. The sauce should be tart, the flavour zesty. Sieve and chill.

To serve the charlotte, remove it from the refrigerator about half an hour before slicing – unless the day is very hot. Trim away any excess cake, run the round edge of a knife blade around the inside of the tin, and turn the loaf onto a platter. With a very sharp knife, cut into $1\frac{1}{2}$ cm/$\frac{1}{2}$ in slices and give two of these per person, overlapped on a dessert plate, with a bit of the sauce napped over. Adorn each plate with a strawberry or two.

Nourishing lunch on a cold day
for eight

ERWTENSOEP
Dutch pea soup

BREAD AND BUTTER PUDDING

BERTHA'S DREAMS

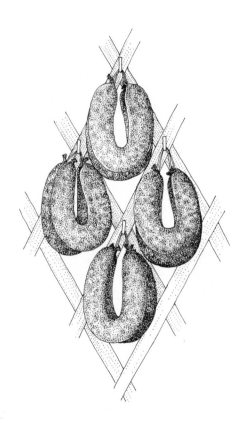

Nourishing lunch on a cold day
for eight

Finesse is not the aim here – just plenty to eat after vigorous football, shovelling snow, or a tough bout of Saturday shopping in winter.

Richard Wiersum, who is Dutch, sent us a handful of traditional recipes from Holland, some of which appear periodically on the menu of his parents' hotel there. Several of these we found curious. The oddest is on page 134; the most orthodox – and comforting – is this *erwtensoep* or "pea soup" with smoked sausage and vegetables, described by Richard as *the* "traditional Dutch dish", and certainly a meal-in-one. The vital secret ingredient is black treacle or molasses. As an alternative, the sheep's head pie on page 197, or *bawd bree*, the Scots hare soup (page 202) – but notice that both those recipes are for 6 people.

Soup is followed by the second quintessentially English pudding of the book, not "summer" but the smooth custard of "bread and butter", given to us by Pamela Vandyke Price. Her recipes, she writes, "tend to be for very plain and simple things". Would there were more cooks in that excellent vein!

After such a meal, some will fall asleep, others return to shovelling snow, and one or two can wrap up the afternoon baking Bertha's dreams, the rich browned-butter cookies sent by Barbara Holland, whose Swedish–American cook made them regularly for two generations of Holland children.

Erwtensoep is the kind of dish to have simmering in various stages half the morning while you do other things; the pudding is prepared several hours ahead and put into the oven just before you serve the soup. Make the cookies while somebody reads to you!

AWS

34

It is significant that each contributor to this robust meal is a northerner. On icy, hardworking days, you don't worry overmuch about subtle partnerships of wine and food; whatever the company feels will be warming is probably best. Of course, the Dutch love red burgundy and can't get enough of it, so an inexpensive rully or mâcon rouge might well be a logical choice with *erwtensoep*.

What to drink with the bread and butter pudding is an interesting question which the distinguished Pamela has omitted to tackle. Again, we hesitate to dogmatise, but if a glass of bual madeira happens to be at hand it will be welcomed.

HD-M

Erwtensoep

This makes a vast amount, reheats well and is certainly delicious.

420 g/14 oz split peas
720 g/1½ lb piece of bacon-cured hock, from pig's hind or fore leg, soaked for several hours in water if you think the meat will be too salty
2 bay leaves
1 heart of celery
2 large onions
1 each large carrot and leek

2 large potatoes
1 handful parsley, without stalks
1 or 2 smoked sausages, weighing about 720 g/1½ lb in all
Pumpernickel or other rye bread, or whole meal bread
Molasses or black treacle
Salt and pepper
Mustard

Soak the peas overnight in water to cover.

Put the hock into a very large stock-pot or saucepan and cover it with about 2½ litres/4¼ pints/2¾ quarts fresh water. Bring this slowly to the simmer, skim, add bay leaves, and barely simmer for 2 hours, or until the ham is tender when pierced with a skewer. If the ham's broth is now too salty, replace some of it with fresh water.

Meanwhile, cut up the celery heart, peel and slice onions, peel and slice carrot into lengths, rinse, trim and slice leek, peel potatoes and cut them into small blocks. Wash parsley and chop it very coarsely.

Drain the peas and add them to the hock's pot; bring the water back to the boil and skim thoroughly. Add all the other vegetables and parsley and simmer for 5 minutes; add the sausage and simmer, stirring occasionally, for 15 minutes more, or till all vegetables are cooked.

Cut a slice of bread per soup bowl, put 1 slice into each, and a dollop of molasses or black treacle atop the bread.

Taste the soup for seasoning, add pepper, and salt if necessary, remove the bay leaves, slice the ham and sausage and put a few slices of both into each bowl. Cover with the soup and vegetables and serve immediately, with mustard.

Richard Wiersum, Surrey, England

Bread and butter pudding

Pamela V. P. doesn't give quantities for this recipe "as her mother used to make it", and proportions for such puddings are indeed better judged by eye than by weight. The tangy marmalade is an unusual detail that makes a striking difference.

Soft butter, unsalted if possible
Sultanas or raisins
Light brown sugar
Unsliced day-old white bread with
 a good crust
Bitter, chunky orange marmalade,
 home-made if possible

Grated nutmeg
3 eggs
1–2 egg yolks
Approximately 750 ml/1¼ pints/3
 cups milk, possibly more

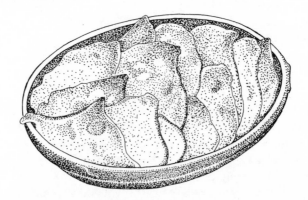

Butter a large shallow ovenproof dish of about 1200 ml/2 pints/5 cups capacity. Sprinkle a few sultanas and a little brown sugar over the bottom.

Slice the bread as thin as possible and don't remove its crusts. Butter enough slices to cover the bottom of the dish, cut each slice into a pair of triangles, and arrange these, butter side up and slightly overlapping, in one layer. Make a second layer of triangles, unbuttered but spread with marmalade. Repeat the layers until the dish is almost full, finishing with bread and butter topped with marmalade and a sprinkling of brown sugar and nutmeg.

Thoroughly whisk the eggs, egg yolks, and milk, and slowly pour enough of this down the side of the dish to reach but not cover the top layer of bread. Bake in the middle of a 180°C/350°F/gas mark 4 oven for about 45 minutes, or until the top has risen and turned a crisp golden-brown.

Serve hot; remainders are tasty eaten cold.

Pamela Vandyke Price, London, England

Bertha's dreams

Makes 5–6 dozen cookies that freeze well.

240 g/8 oz butter, unsalted if
   possible
35 blanched almonds
150 g/5 oz/¾ cup castor
   (granulated) sugar

10 ml/2 teasp vanilla extract
300 g/10 oz/2 cups plain flour
One 5-ml spoon/1 teasp baking
   powder
Salt

Lightly butter several heavy baking sheets.

Brown the 240 g/8 oz butter to a pale nutty colour in a small saucepan, remove quickly from the heat, once coloured, to prevent burning, and pour into a medium mixing bowl. Put the bowl into cold water to speed the butter's cooling. Meanwhile sliver the almonds.

Beat sugar into the butter, followed by vanilla extract. Sieve together the flour, baking powder and, if the butter is unsalted, a pinch of salt. Sift the dry ingredients over the butter base, mix, and blend the dough until smooth.

Refrigerate if necessary to firm, break off bits of dough and roll them between your fingers into balls of 2½ cm/1 in diameter. Place the balls, well-spaced, on baking sheets and firmly press a sliver of blanched almond into the top of each.

Bake cookies in a 155°C/310°F/gas mark 2 oven for about 30 minutes or until golden-brown. Cool on racks and store in airtight tins.

Barbara D. Holland, Columbus, Ohio Wine & Food Society, USA

An unorthodox luncheon at Christmas
for six

CÔTE DE BŒUF, SAUCE VIN ROUGE, SAUCE POIVRE VERT
Wing ribs, red wine and green peppercorn sauces

ROAST JERUSALEM ARTICHOKES
CUCUMBERS WITH GARLIC AND MINT

BOMBE À LA LORRAINE, GRAND MARNIER SAUCE

CRYSTALLISED ORANGE PEEL

DARK FRUIT-CAKE

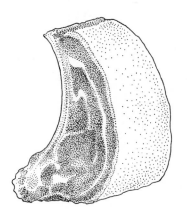

An unorthodox luncheon at Christmas
for six

There are times when you don't want the full Dickensian Christmas story of three generations at table, the huge turkey, cranberry sauce, mince pies and days of leftovers. So this is a small and *soigné* meal with a minimum of last-minute preparation and the aim that you all rise able-bodied from the match.

Straight into the main course: Lyn Hall's glorious beef ribs, served – we hope – rare as beef should be. We ourselves have taken to beef at Christmas, with a sauce of white wine and Stilton cheese, and we like Lyn's red wine and green pepper alternatives. It's Lyn who gave us the excellent tip – explained here and recurring throughout the book – on re-heating carved meat without further cooking it.

For inhabitants of the northern hemisphere, as a change from beef-plus-roast-potatoes there is the more interesting flavour of knobbly Jerusalem artichokes – neither artichokes nor Middle Eastern, but a North American vegetable whose name derives from *girasole*, the Italian for sunflower, to a species of which this plant is the tuber. With it, the snap of garlicked and vinegared cucumber.

Dessert is a layering of frozen creams, like unwrapping extra Christmas presents: chocolate or coffee, and orange, plus a frothing Grand Marnier custard sauce. And then with coffee, the simplicity of crystallised orange peel.

Helene Bennett's dark fruit-cake is ready to fill any gap in the appetite that might open late afternoon. She "lost" one such in a cupboard for two years, drenched it with several ounces of spirit on rediscovery, and found the result "better than ever". Carole Collier of New York sent us a similar recipe.

Almost everything here can be made ahead, and the fruit-cake *must* have six weeks' advantage. The beef and artichokes are the only aspects to be cooked from scratch in the hour before you sit down, and the beef can wait quite a while to be carved.

AWS

We have not usually concerned ourselves in this book with aperitifs, as most people have clear ideas as to what best whets their appetites, but Christmas is special. The hours before the meal are likely to have passed in some pleasurable – even religious – activity, so most of us are happy to spend an hour relaxing with agreeable companions, glass in hand, before the serious business begins.

Of course, there's always champagne, but you might be adventurous and try what is currently the most popular cocktail in France, *le champagne framboise*: a spoonful of raspberry liqueur in an icy glass of the wine. You can spend a pleasant few minutes experimenting as to how large a spoonful this ought to be. Alternatively, a top quality young fino sherry, served very cold. Or simply your favourite dry white wine.

But, ah, the roast! A bottle of the best here, and for most of us – *pace* our German members! – this will be something red and rich. If your "cellar" (which in a modern house is probably a space under the stairs) contains any fine cabernet sauvignon, whether from a great Napa domaine like Mondavi or Montelena, from Australia's Tahbilk or Lake's Folly, from South Africa's Stellenbosch, or from one of the

classic Bordeaux growths, we hope you brought up the bottles a fortnight ago, so they can now be decanted. How many hours ahead to do this causes endless discussion among IWFS members. We'll simply say that if the wine is very old, play safe: open the bottles and decant just before you sit down.

It's hard to match *any* wine to the flavours of chocolate or coffee, even more so if either is part of an ice cream. When we tested this meal, we just skipped wine with dessert. But the fruit-cake seemed to take wings when married to a glass of port – not our usual teatime drink, but this *is* Christmas! If you have a good vintage, bring it up out of storage early in December. Latterly, however, producers have been concentrating on old tawnies which have no sediment so can be served as soon as bought; some of these are very fine. Last Christmas we particularly liked Berry Bros & Rudd's Wm Pickering, produced in 1982 to celebrate 250 years in the same London shop. But there is a chauvinist in all of us, and this does seem the moment to bolster one's Christmas contentment with the local version of "port" – whether made in New Zealand, Australia or the United States (but not, please, in Britain!)

HD-M

Côte de bœuf

Ask your butcher for two ribs of prime beef on the bone, to serve six. The two which meet the sirloin (short loin), known in England as wing ribs and containing part of the "eye", are the tenderest and most succulent. Ask him to chine them for easier carving, to remove the gristle, and skewer fat to meat at the wide end so that the fat won't shrink. If the butcher does not hang his beef, keep the ribs for a week in your refrigerator.

When ready to roast, bring the meat to room temperature, trim of excess fat if necessary, and rub the flesh with a cut clove of garlic and some black pepper. Turn your grill or broiler on to full heat for 15 minutes before use. A strong gas grill or a radiant electric one in a modern half-oven works best.

Salt the meat, rub it with peanut oil and place it to sear, first on one side and then the other, about 8 cm/3 in from the heat. Then move the ribs to a distance of 13 cm/5 in away to finish cooking and avoid burning the exterior; for rare, allow a total of 5–7 minutes per side. Timing depends on the power of your grill.

If you think that this won't be suitable here, roast the beef for 20 minutes in a 245°C/475°F/gas mark 9 oven, reduce the heat to 165°C/325°F/gas mark 3 and roast for about 20 minutes longer, or until the meat tests done to the required degree.

Test it, for the following information, by pressing the centre of the "eye" with your thumb:

- Meat spongy and soft, indentation of thumb remains – very rare
- Slightest resistance to thumb – rare
- Greater resistance – medium rare
- Thumb meets firm resistance and causes no indentation – well-done

Well-done meat is best finished in a hot oven after the formation of a good crust, or the outside will toughen and turn black. If some guests like rare meat and others well-done, grill the ribs rare and carve them. Return potentially well-done slices to the grill and in a few minutes they will be thoroughly cooked.

In any case, allow the ribs to rest intact for at least 20 minutes in a warm place. If you want to reheat slices once carved, align them on a platter, cover the surface with a wet and wrung-out tea-towel and place the platter under the grill or broiler until the towel begins to steam. This will heat the meat without further browning. Serve with the following sauces.

Sauce vin rouge

2 shallots
Butter
480 ml/16 fl oz/2 cups very lightly salted meat broth, of good colour (page 220)
75 ml/5 tbs armagnac or other brandy
90 ml/3 fl oz/generous ⅓ cup tawny port

330 ml/11 fl oz/generous 1⅓ cup hearty red wine
One 5-ml spoon/1 teasp poivre vert (green peppercorns)
Salt, if necessary
Two 5-ml spoons/2 teasp arrowroot
5 ml/1 teasp each lemon juice and tawny port

Peel and mince the shallots, sauté them in a little butter until golden-brown, place them in a saucepan with the broth – strained through a double thickness of muslin or cheesecloth – the spirits (except for the spoonful of port), and wine; reduce until you have 360 ml/12 fl oz/1½ cups. Remove any surface scum. Wash the *poivre vert* and put it through a sieve; add to the sauce and check the seasoning.

All can be prepared in advance to this point and finished as follows shortly before serving. Dissolve arrowroot in the lemon juice and remaining port, add it to the sauce, and simmer for about a minute. The result should be dark and glossy. Taste again for seasoning, and strain.

Sauce poivre vert

To half the *sauce vin rouge*, add one 15-ml spoon/1 tbs washed and sieved green peppercorns, and more whole ones, to taste, just before serving.

Lyn Hall, Richmond, Surrey, England

Roast Jerusalem artichokes

If you don't have, or can't buy, good beef dripping, then forget the roasting and boil these, whole and unpeeled, in acidulated water for about 15 minutes, drain well and turn them in plenty of unsalted butter to serve.

720 g/1½ lb Jerusalem artichokes,   Good beef dripping from your own
    not too large and of uniform size   roast or bought from the butcher
                                        Salt and pepper

Scrub the artichokes under water with a brush, cut off any tails but leave the skins on. Put the tubers in a single layer in a wide, shallow baking dish with just enough dripping to coat the vegetables, plus a bit more. Add salt and roast them, uncovered, high in a 180°C/350°F/gas mark 4 oven for about 45 minutes – basting occasionally – or until soft and almost melting in the middle. If you are roasting rather than grilling the meat, put the artichokes into the beef's oven when its temperature is lowered to 165°C/325°F/gas mark 3, turn up the oven when the meat comes out, and finish off the artichokes while the beef is resting.

Drain, season, and serve.

An alternative, for a simpler meal, is to wrap half the artichokes in narrow strips of bacon, secured with small skewers, and roast as above.

Cucumbers with garlic and mint

The authors of Mastering the Art of French Cooking put us on to the technique of salting cucumbers to expel their moisture while improving the flavour with vinegar; it is far preferable to blanching this watery vegetable. The six cloves of garlic mellow significantly in cooking. We seem to be able to buy cucumbers in most places all year round now, and they are an unexpected Christmas vegetable.

1400 g/3 lb cucumbers, unpeeled	*6 cloves garlic*
weight	*About 24 fresh mint leaves or one*
60 ml/4 tbs wine vinegar	*2.5-ml spoon/½ teasp dried mint*
Two 5-ml spoons/2 teasp salt	*60 g/2 oz butter*
One 1.25-ml spoon/¼ teasp	*Pepper*
granulated sugar	

Peel the cucumbers, cut them across into halves if long, then in half lengthwise and scrape out the seeds with a small spoon. Cut into strips of 1½ cm/½ in wide and the strips into 4 cm/1½ in lengths. Put the cucumbers into a large, wide china bowl or two smaller ones, and toss them with the vinegar, salt, and sugar. Let the salt work for an hour or more as you toss the mixture regularly, then drain the cucumbers and pat them dry with kitchen paper. Under no circumstances rinse them – the salt and vinegar will *make* the flavour.

Put the cucumbers into a wide, shallow, and heavy baking dish, add the peeled, sliced garlic, the shredded fresh mint or the crumbled dry, the butter and *no* salt, and bake them uncovered in the middle of a 180°C/350°F/gas mark 4 oven, with Jerusalem artichokes above if you like, for about an hour, perhaps more, tossing and basting at intervals until the cucumbers are tender. They should still have a crunch, reinforced by the vinegar's acid, and will be turning golden. Add pepper – salt will almost certainly not be needed – and toss.

These can be prepared ahead of time, cooled uncovered, and reheated with a drop of water in a covered saucepan atop the stove if you wish. This approach is certainly better if you are *roasting* the meat.

Bombe à la Lorraine

Named for the shape of its high, bullet-like mould, a *bombe* means a de luxe package of ice creams, fun for the maker, and a surprise for the guests.

900–1050 g/30–35 oz of the best	*2 eggs*
chocolate or coffee ice cream	*2 egg yolks*
90 g/3 oz butter, unsalted if possible	

270 g/9 oz/1⅓ cups castor
  (granulated) sugar
The grated zest of one orange

30 ml/2 tbs each Grand Marnier
  liqueur and fresh orange juice
A bar of hard, semi-sweet
  chocolate

Lightly oil a *bombe* or jelly mould that will hold about 2 litres/3¼ pints/2 quarts liquid – or, lacking either, a stainless steel mixing bowl of the same capacity; the latter, however, won't give as smart a result. Using a metal spoon, line it with a 2½ cm/1 in layer of slightly softened chocolate or coffee ice cream. Reserve the remaining ice cream in the freezer, and freeze the mould for 2–3 hours or until the contents are firm.

Prepare an orange custard for the centre by melting the butter in a heavy saucepan. Beat the eggs and yolks in a bowl, add the sugar and zest of orange and whisk for several minutes until the eggs thicken considerably; beat in the liqueur and the melted butter. Turn this back into the saucepan and whisk over a moderate heat until the custard thickens enough to coat a spoon, which will be just before the boiling point. Quickly strain the custard into a chilled bowl, add orange juice and whisk. When completely cold, pour into the lined mould and freeze overnight.

The next day, cover custard with the reserved ice cream, a bit softened, smooth the surface and cover all with foil and the mould's lid if you have it, and refreeze.

The *bombe* can be made up to a week ahead of serving. Thirty to forty-five minutes before this moment, remove the lid and foil from the mould, wrap the *bombe* in a hot and wrung-out towel, and ease the ice cream onto a serving plate. Put this into the refrigerator until you're ready to present it. To do so, surround the *bombe* with some chocolate curls made by running a swivel vegetable peeler along the edges of the semi-sweet bar that's been slightly warmed by the heat of your hand.

Slice the *bombe* at the table, and pass it with the warm Grand Marnier sauce.

Grand Marnier sauce

120 g/4 oz butter, unsalted if
  possible
2 eggs
150 g/5 oz/¾ cup castor
  (granulated) sugar

60 ml/4 tbs Grand Marnier, or to
  taste
120 ml/4 fl oz/½ cup fresh orange
  juice

Make this exactly as for the orange custard above, and as you will probably want to prepare the sauce early, reheat it carefully in a *bain-marie*.

Lorraine Gillespie, Edmonton, Alberta Wine & Food Society, Canada

Crystallised orange peel

5 large oranges
240 ml/8 fl oz/1 cup water
either   *90 ml/3 fl oz/generous*
              ⅓ cup liquid glucose
              and 60 g/2
              oz/generous ¼ cup
              granulated sugar

or (USA) 60 ml/2 fl oz/¼ cup
              light corn syrup and
              390 g/13 oz/scant 2
              cups granulated
              sugar
210 g/7 oz/1 cup granulated sugar
for coating peels

Cut the oranges in half across and squeeze out as much juice as possible; refrigerate this to drink, or use it for the *bombe à la Lorraine*. Cut the peel halves across.

Bring them to the boil in a large saucepan of water, simmer for 10 minutes, drain and repeat the process twice more with fresh water, simmering the peels for a total of 30–40 minutes, until tender. The repeated blanching extracts bitter oils.

Drain the peels and scrape away their excess pulp.

In the same saucepan, combine the measured water, the glucose or corn syrup and the appropriate amount of sugar, and swirl these over a low heat until the sugar dissolves. Bring the syrup to the boil and boil it without stirring to reach the soft ball stage, which registers 113°C/235°F on a candy thermometer.

Add the peel and barely simmer it for 30–40 minutes, stirring frequently to prevent scorching, until it becomes translucent.

Turn peel and syrup into a bowl, cool and let stand overnight, covered, in a cool, dry place.

The following day, remove the peel from its syrup and drain for 3 hours on wire racks. With scissors, cut the pieces into strips ¾ cm/¼ in wide. Roll these in the extra sugar to coat well, and place them to dry on clean racks for another 3 hours. Roll in sugar again.

Can be stored in an airtight container for a long time.

Richard S. Webster, Northern Illinois Wine & Food Society, USA

Dark fruit-cake

450 g/15 oz dark seedless raisins
480 ml/16 fl oz/2 cups water
345 g/11½ oz/ 1¾ cups granulated
  sugar
120 g/4 oz butter, preferably
  unsalted
1 large egg
450 g/15 oz/3 cups plain flour
One 5-ml spoon/1 teasp each salt,
  baking soda, ground allspice,
  ground cinnamon

480 g/1 lb mixed candied – but
not crystallised – fruits and
peels, such as whole cherries in
different colours, plus pineapple
rings and citron slices cut up
coarsely
240 g/8 oz broken walnuts or
  pecans
90 ml/3 fl oz/generous ⅜ cup
  cognac, rum, or bourbon whiskey
Extra spirits for ripening

Butter a 25 cm/10 in round cake tin with a central tube, or a 25 cm/10 in spring-form or ordinary metal cake tin, or two loaf tins of 480 g/1 lb capacity each, or four little loaf tins, and line bottom and sides of each with a double thickness of buttered greaseproof or parchment paper cut to extend 5 cm/2 in above the tins to protect cake tops from excessive browning.

Boil together, for 3 minutes, the raisins, water, sugar, and butter. Let stand until cool, whisk the egg and beat it in.

Sift the dry ingredients twice, mix them with the candied fruits and nuts, combine with the raisin mixture and whatever spirit you choose. Pour the batter into tin or tins, rap each smartly on the work surface to settle the contents, and make a smooth hollow in or along the centre of each so that cakes will rise evenly. Bake them in a 155°C/310°F/gas mark 2 oven. A 25 cm/10 in tin takes about 3 hours; the smaller pans 2–2½ hours and 1¼–1¾ hours respectively. They are done when a trussing needle thrust into the centres tests clean and hot.

Cool the cakes on racks, in their tins, for about half an hour, then remove and anoint them well with the same spirit as used in the batter. When cold, wrap them in greaseproof or parchment paper and then in foil and store in sealed tins. Douse with spirits twice more at two-week intervals, then wrap and store the cakes for at least six weeks.

Being heavy and rich, this recipe makes up to fifty servings. After the cake has been opened and used, refresh the remainder with more spirits before packing it away again.

Helene Bennett, New York Wine & Food Society, USA

Dinners and Suppers

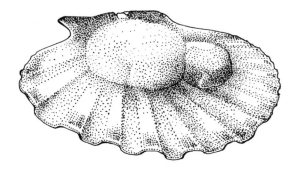

A Southern family feast

for ten

GOOTSIE'S CONCH OR "CRAWFISH" CHOWDER

CHAMPAGNE-BRAISED HAM
CHAMPAGNE AND TARRAGON SAUCE

GREENS AND OKRA
BOURBON SWEET POTATOES

KENTUCKY CHESS PIE

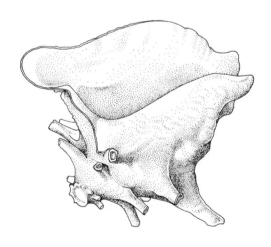

A Southern family feast
for ten

We're making free now with this word "dinner", letting it straddle the mid-afternoon in the Southern American fashion of late family lunches, starting maybe at 2 o'clock on a Sunday and going on for hours. A big, leisurely meal expressing the unrushed hospitality of the South and the stylish eating which has always characterised the more affluent tables of that region – perhaps better than in any other part of the United States.

And unlike the preceding Christmas lunch, this is one of those times to eat lots, revel in the leftovers – and hang the expense, which, come to think of it, you've already done for the Christmas menu. The month here would be March, for those north of the Equator, and September for the folk below.

Gootsie's chowder of conch, or "crawfish", from Perrine Palmer of Miami Beach – using Florida coast seafood – is one of the pedigreed East-coast American chowders or fish stews, started off by the frying of salt pork and onion and finished with the quick cooking of local seafood: clams and oysters in the North, shrimp or oysters further South, with other fish coming in as caught. Chowder is served as a meal-in-one, or as here, a first course. If you think it's too much – and it *is* copious, and pricey to make – reduce the quantities.

The *plat de résistance* isn't really Southern in treatment, but, inspired by the famous Southern country hams – a different cure in each state – and by Southerners' partiality to the bubbles of champagne, we thought it appropriate. The sauce, redolent of the ham's goodness, is infused with tarragon and finished with a little cream.

Vegetables – the greens and okra – are typically Southern and "soul"

52

or Southern black in origin, but cooked more simply – and the greens much faster – than is usual there. These go side by side with Sarah Staton's sweet potatoes, mashed and whipped with butter and bourbon and brown sugar – the "real thing" according to our Southern sources – as directed by Mrs Staton's Kentucky mother and grandmother for as long as she can remember.

If you're still conscious at this stage, the dessert is Kentucky chess pie, another recipe from Sarah Staton's grandmother and perhaps the ultimate manifestation of the Southern sweet tooth – unless that status be challenged by the better-known pecan pie.

For this feast, you will *work*, and indeed for much of it at the last minute, but then dining on such a scale is nowadays a rare thing. The chowder should be done at one go, while the ham is braising. Have an interval then, after eating the fish, while the ham rests and you make the sauce and bake the potatoes (previously boiled, puréed, and casseroled) and cook greens and okra. The pie, whose pastry can be mixed the night before, should be baked some time in the morning.

AWS

Elizabeth Kivlan of New York, who was born in Rome, Georgia (and has a lovely accent to prove it) reckons that to start this meal in proper style, you should precede it with a glass of bourbon and "branch water" – "branch" in old-fashioned Southern lingo being a fork of the local stream, and its water simply *water* – some pink champagne, or a mint julep. If the latter is your choice, we do *not* recommend the old custom of serving one large bowlful and a lot of straws; in an atmosphere less gracious than that of the South, this might create enmities! We do, however, approve of the handled glasses sometimes used for julep, which should be kept as cool as the verse of John Milton:

> . . . behold this cordial julep here
> That foams and dances in his crystal bounds
> With spirits of balm and fragrant syrups mix'd.

A fine partner for the chowder would be verdelho madeira or a chilled Napa chardonnay. Southerners particularly enjoy pink wines, says Elizabeth, so we propose one with the ham. But beware: as Serena Sutcliffe remarks in her excellent *Wine Drinker's Handbook*, "a rosé is not a rosé is not a rosé", so choose carefully. Henri Maire's from Arbois in the Jura would work well, as would a Napa grignolino rosé. For a meal like this, some Southerners serve goblets of iced water or iced, mint-sprigged tea and dispense with wine altogether.

The chess pie is too sweet for anything but a glass of cold milk, but black coffee sipped with a digestif of Southern Comfort liqueur would make a splendid finale. Or, if you still have the energy, you might mix a Rhett Butler – equal parts of curaçao, Southern Comfort and citrus juices, topped with a splash of soda. With respect to Colonel Saunders (whose work I admire), all this adds up to something a bit fancier than fried chicken and Coke.

HD-M

Gootsie's conch or "crawfish" chowder

The conch – pronounced, we gather, "conk" – is a large mollusc whose exuberantly vulgar spiral shell, shaded from pale orange to deep pink and rippling with spikes, is the American classic in which to hear the sea's roar. Its flesh, described by the late Waverley Root as tasting "like a slightly exotic clam", is firm and sweet, and the beast is found in Floridian waters and throughout the Caribbean and Gulf of Mexico. Whelks, another marine snail but living in cooler waters on both sides of the Atlantic, can substitute.

"Crawfish" is a colloquial misnomer for the saltwater crustacean called spiny lobster or *langouste* – not to be confused with freshwater crayfish or *écrevisse*. The spiny lobster – without claws and large in the tail – seems to swim off diverse coasts; those round Florida, Jamaica, California, the Mediterranean, Brazil, South and West Africa spring to mind.

If none of these seafoods is available, substitute the flesh of "breakers", trade name for true lobsters, or *homards*, of the powerful claws.

120 g/4 oz salted belly or flank pork (salt pork)	*4 medium carrots*
	4 stalks celery
2 medium onions	*1 large sweet green pepper*

4 large cloves garlic
600 g/20 oz of good canned
    tomatoes, including their juices
90 g/3 oz concentrated tomato
    paste
15 ml/1 tbs wine vinegar
5 bay leaves
30 ml/2 tbs barbecue sauce, if
    available
Two 5-ml spoons/2 teasp dried
    basil

One 5-ml spoon/1 teasp salt
5 ml/1 teasp tabasco sauce
2 large potatoes
10 large conches or whelks,
    skinned and uncooked,
    or 5 live spiny lobsters weighing
    about 720 g/1½ lb apiece; if
    both conches and spiny
    lobsters are available, use
    some of each
Pepper

Dice the salt pork, and render it down in one very large or two smaller stock-pots or saucepans until the meat is crisp and the fat has melted.

Meanwhile, peel and finely dice the onions and carrots, dice the celery and the peppers' flesh, minus its core and seeds, peel and mince the garlic. Sauté these in the rendered fat until softened.

Pour 2 litres/3¼ pints/2 quarts water into the pot(s), bring to the boil, add the tomatoes and tomato paste and mix well. Add the vinegar, bay leaves, barbecue sauce, basil, salt, and tabasco, bring back to the boil, and simmer gently, partially covered, for 1½ hours. Cool slightly and degrease.

Meanwhile, if you think the conch or whelks will be tough, wrap them in cheesecloth or muslin and beat them with a mallet to tenderise. Cut the flesh into ¾ × 1½ cm/¼ × ½ in pieces and reserve. If using spiny lobsters, kill them by severing the spinal cord and cutting each lobster in half lengthwise. Remove the flesh from the shells, de-vein and cut it into bite-size chunks. Reserve. (The lobster shells can be used to make, say, a lobster bisque, which then can be frozen for future use).

Peel the potatoes and dice them into ¾ cm/¼ in squares; add these to the chowder base and simmer for 15 minutes.

Add the pieces of conch, stir, and simmer for 5 minutes more or till the fish is tender – if overcooked it toughens. Treat lobster the same, simmering for 5–10 minutes until done.

Fish out the bay leaves if possible, check the seasoning, grind on copious black pepper and serve the chowder in deep bowls.

Perrine Palmer, Miami, Florida Wine & Food Society, USA

Champagne-braised ham, champagne and tarragon sauce

An unusual treatment for ham, using champagne or any dry *méthode champenoise* wine such as *cava* – from Catalonia in Northern Spain – Californian Schramsberg, or Australian Seaview Brut. This yields a vast quantity, as a ham should, so you'll be able to send the meat round hot and eat it cold on subsequent days.

4 large carrots
2 large onions
2 leeks
Butter and oil
A boiled ham, skinned and largely de-fatted, weighing 4¼–4¾ kg/9–10 lb
A few parsley stalks

1 bay leaf
2 sprigs thyme
900 ml/1½ pints/1 quart champagne or méthode champenoise wine, plus more at the end
600 ml/1 pint/2½ cups meat broth (page 220)

Sauce
Braising liquid from the ham
30 ml/2 tbs brandy
One 5-ml spoon/1 teasp dried tarragon

300 ml/½ pint/1¼ cups thick cream, plus more if required
1½ × 15-ml spoons/1½ tbs cornflour (cornstarch)
Salt and pepper

Peel and slice the carrots and onions, trim and slice the leeks. In a heavy cocotte or casserole large enough to take the ham, melt a little butter with some oil and sauté the vegetables gently until softened and just browning. Place the ham, fat side up, atop the vegetables, add herbs, champagne, and broth. Bring the liquid to a simmer atop the stove, cover the casserole with foil, and place it in a 165°C/325°F/gas mark 3 oven. Keep the liquid at the shuddering point for 1½–2 hours, basting the ham well every 30 minutes. It is cooked when a skewer pierces the thickest part without much resistance.

Drain the ham and let it rest in a warm place for half an hour before carving. If it must be held longer, put it, loosely covered with foil, into the turned-off oven with the door ajar for up to an hour.

Meanwhile, prepare the sauce by straining and degreasing the braising liquid and reducing it over a high heat to about 600 ml/1 pint/2½ cups. Add the brandy and boil it for about 2 minutes to vaporise the alcohol. Strain into a heavy saucepan and add the tarragon and all but 30 ml/2 tbs of the cream. Simmer for two or three minutes, then slowly add the cornflour previously diluted in the reserved cream. Simmer the sauce until thick enough barely to coat the back of a spoon. Dilute with more cream if necessary, and add a final splash of champagne to sharpen the outcome.

Correct seasoning of the sauce, carve the ham onto a heated platter, reheating if necessary as in the recipe for *côte de bœuf* on page 42, and serve with the sauce in one or two warmed boats.

Greens and okra

Take about 1600 g/3½ lb of greens – spring greens, the leaves of Swiss chard, cabbage, or collards (a Southern American type of cabbage brought there from Africa) – wash, stem where necessary, and trim them; shred them thin and boil in a little salted water until cooked – different greens will take varying amounts of time. Drain, toss in butter over a medium heat, season, and present the greens in a hot dish.

Take 1 kg/2¼ lbs of okra, cut off the stems and slice the vegetables across into thin rings. Melt 60 g/2 oz butter in a heavy saucepan, add the okra with salt and steam it, covered, for 10 to 15 minutes or until tender, stirring occasionally. Uncover and turn the heat up; toss the okra a few times to colour. Correct seasoning and serve.

Bourbon sweet potatoes

1900 g/4 lb sweet potatoes or
   yams
120 ml/4 fl oz/½ cup melted butter
60 ml/4 tbs, more or less,
   Kentucky bourbon
75 ml/5 tbs orange juice

60 g/2 oz/⅓ cup dark brown sugar
A 1.25-ml spoon/¼ teasp grated
   nutmeg or ground cinnamon
A pinch of salt
120 g/4 oz coarsely-chopped
   pecans or walnuts

Wash the potatoes, cut off the tips and quarter them, unpeeled. Cook the quarters, covered, in boiling salted water for 10–15 minutes, or until tender when pierced with a skewer. Drain and skin and put them through a ricer, or mash them with a potato masher.

Whip the purée smooth and beat in all the remaining ingredients. Taste, correct seasoning, and pour into a 2½ litre/4 pint/2½ quart buttered casserole.

While the ham is resting, bake the casserole in a 180°C/350°F/gas mark 4 oven for 20–30 minutes or until the potatoes are hot through.

Sarah Staton, Palm Beach, Florida Wine & Food Society, USA

Kentucky chess pie

This very sweet dessert has many variations which have long been popular in the South. We've heard of a version called Tyler pudding pie, named for President John Tyler, a Virginian, and another with nuts, raisins, and dates, called Jefferson Davis pie to honour the Confederate president.

Some chess pies harbour lemon juice or buttermilk or brown sugar, or lie beneath meringue, and there are several stories to "explain" the name. One has it that "chess" is a corruption of "cheese", after the 18th-century lemon curd or "cheese" cakes from which some say chess pies are descended. But we prefer the yarn supplied by Mrs Staton, in which unexpected company is said to have dropped in on a household whose black cook improvised a pastry filled with eggs, butter, and flavouring. When asked for the name of the mixture, she answered softly, "Jes' pie".

As this recipe is rich, you may find that one 23–25 cm/9–10 in pie is enough, after such a blow-out, to provide ten modest pieces. If you think not, make two pies.

Pastry
225 g/7½ oz/1½ cups plain flour
A large pinch of salt

90 g/3 oz firm lard or similar
   shortening
Iced water

Filling
30 g/1 oz butter, softened
285 g/9½ oz/1½ cups castor
  (granulated) sugar

Two 5-ml spoons/2 teasp plain
  flour

One 5-ml spoon/1 teasp white corn   5 ml/1 teasp vanilla extract
   or maize meal, finely-ground   One scant 1.25-ml spoon/scant ¼
4 eggs   teasp grated nutmeg
60 ml/4 tbs milk

To make the pastry, sift together the flour and salt, dice the lard and cut or rub it deftly into the flour until the mixture looks like small peas. Sprinkle on about 30 ml/2 tbs iced water and bring the pastry together into a dough that just holds its form, adding more water if necessary. Wrap the dough in paper and a plastic bag and refrigerate it for several hours or overnight.

Let the pastry come to room temperature, roll it out and line a 23–25 cm/9–10 in metal pie dish or a flan ring set onto a heavy baking sheet. Refrigerate for half an hour, then line the shell with paper or foil weighted with coins or dried beans and half-bake it, "blind", in a 180°C/350°F/gas mark 4 oven for about 20 minutes or until the pastry has set and just begun to colour.

To make the filling, cream together the butter, sugar, flour, and corn meal. Beat the eggs and combine them with milk, vanilla, and nutmeg; add this slowly to the sugar and flour, beat, and pour the filling into its shell. Grate more nutmeg on top.

Place the pie in the lower third of a 230°C/450°F/gas mark 8 oven and immediately reduce the heat to 205°C/400°F/gas mark 6. Bake for 10 minutes and reduce the heat to 155°C/310°F/gas mark 2 and bake for 20–30 minutes more or until the filling is golden-brown and puffed. Cool on a rack and serve the pie at room temperature.

Sarah Staton

An evening with Lur Saluces
for four

CANARD À LA FAÇON ALEXANDRE DE LUR SALUCES
Duck with fresh orange juice

LES PRIMEURS
Early vegetables

CRÉMANT SORBET

CŒURS À LA CRÈME, SALADE VERTE
Hearts of cream, green salad

TARTE TATIN AUX POIRES
Upside-down pear tart

An evening with Lur Saluces
for four

Our first true dinner, early summer, and conceived as the setting for a most unconventional French jewel.

Certain splendid wines are rarely brought to the table because one just isn't sure how to drink them, which may explain the eclipse of sauternes. So we were delighted when Howard Meighan, who *is* our New York Society, sent a recipe for roast duck whose distinctive condiments are warm orange juice – as opposed to the ho-hum predictable orange glaze – and chilled Château d'Yquem!

At the time of the Bordeaux 1855 classification, Yquem was designated the finest of all sweet wines, and the accolade remains unchallenged. But the question of who invented this recipe is not resolved – Howard and Alexandre de Lur Saluces, Yquem's owner, each insists it belongs to the other.

The combination is striking and delicious and contains so many elements of surprise that preliminaries are best limited to an unobtrusive glass or two of dry white wine. We rose to the occasion when serving the duck and got out Yquem. A lesser sauternes, which need be no more costly than a modest claret, would suit the moment admirably. With this, on side plates, the young vegetables which the French call *primeurs*, still delicate and slightly sweet in early summer. We've suggested small courgettes and the tiny edible pods known in Europe as *mange-tout* peas and as snow or sugar peas elsewhere. If these are not to be had, substitute young broad beans or the slimmest French beans, tiny carrots or turnips with tops intact, these two quickly cooked in a little water, butter, seasoning, and a pinch of sugar.

Sorbets usually appear after many elaborate courses, but we're moving even further away from convention; a palate cleanser to follow the duck makes a graceful bridge towards the cheese course. The recipe is based on any good, dry and fruity sparkling wine made by the champagne method – hence the name *crémant*. We habitually use the Spanish *cava*.

Our cheese isn't really *fromage*, but heart-shaped *cœurs à la crème*, made of cream, yoghurt, and egg white, which suggest the light acidity of ripe cream cheese. A salad here, and with these fresh tastes, a lively red wine like a young gamay, Italian sangiovese, or a German *rotwein*.

And finally, a variation on the famous upside-down apple tart devised by the Demoiselles Tatin at their inn below Orléans and the River Loire: a *Tatin* of pears whose grainy texture is a foil to its sweet caramel. We had a brain-storming session with Harry Yoxall about what to drink here. Though the pears' baked colour is close to Yquem, to bring that back would be overdoing it. Since the tart is cooked in reverse, someone suggested an Australian white muscat or Porphyry (the sweet dessert wine of New South Wales). Or is it the moment to bring out a crisp English or Oregon apple wine? Or a tiny – and icy – glass of the blended calvados and apple juice that the inhabitants of Normandy have christened Pommeau?

The duck and vegetables need last-minute care, unlike the sorbet, cheese, and salad. The tart can be baked while you eat, wait if necessary, and be turned out when you wish.

AWS and HD-M

Canard à la façon Alexandre de Lur Saluces

In *Julia Child & Company*, J.C. outlines a method of roasting duck in a very slow oven for several hours. We find this works beautifully: the duck emerges tender, slightly pink, and not excessively fatty. We recommend the technique.

A 2–2¼ kg/4½ lb oven-ready never-frozen duckling Salt	A sprig of thyme 1 small onion 2 small oranges

Chop away the duck's wing tips and remove the wishbone if this has not been done already. These can be used, with neck and appropriate giblets, to make a good stock for soup.

Remove fat from the duck's inside, season with salt and thyme; stuff with the peeled, sliced onion. Truss the bird and prick its skin with a sharp fork all over thighs, back, and lower breast. Dry the duck with kitchen paper and place it on a rack inside a roasting tin. Put the tin, uncovered, in the middle of a 115°C/240°F/gas mark ¼ oven for about 3 hours, pricking the bird several times during roasting to release the fat.

Slice the oranges in half across and wrap each half in a small piece of cheesecloth or muslin, fastening it compactly and neatly at the uncut end. During the final 30 minutes of the duck's roasting, heat these in a shallow container on the oven floor.

Duck has reached the pink stage when juices from the fattest part of a thigh are slightly rosy if the flesh is pierced. Remove duck from oven and let the bird rest in a warm place for 10 minutes. Take out trussing strings.

To carve, remove the thighs and drumsticks and cut 4–6 thin slices from each breast. Carve the meat from legs and thighs, and divide among 4 heated plates. (If the duck has cooled in carving, reheat by Lyn Hall's method on page 43). Add an orange half to each plate and serve, accompanied by separate dishes of *primeurs*.

Proceed to eat in the manner prescribed by Howard Meighan:

> Instruct the lucky guests to squeeze the warm orange juice over the meat, having first put aside the duck's skin. Dip fingers into a handy finger bowl of well-iced water to be rid of the orange. Take a first bite and while it is being savoured, drink an appropriate amount of the sauternes – nicely chilled – which the thoughtful host has provided. Between the third and fifth tastes of this delectable medley of flavours it is proper to offer a toast to the Count and Countess de Lur Saluces.

Howard S. Meighan, New York Wine & Food Society, USA

Les primeurs

Mange-tout peas, also known as sugar or snow peas

240/8 oz mange-tout	*A good pinch of sugar*
15 g/½ oz butter	*Salt and pepper*

Courgettes

8 very small courgettes (zucchini)	*Salt and pepper*
15 g/½ oz butter	

Top, tail, and string the peas. Put them into a low-sided heavy saucepan with butter, sugar and a hint of salt. Add enough water to moisten well.

Trim courgettes and slice them across into thin rounds.

While carving the duck, cover peas with a lid and bring them to the simmer. Heat butter for the courgettes in a medium sauté pan, add vegetables and salt. Toss these over a fairly high heat, and periodically shake the saucepan. If you prefer not to do three things at once, keep the carved duck hot on a platter, loosely covered with foil, in a very low oven while cooking the vegetables; or reheat the meat, using Lyn Hall's method, when the vegetables are almost done.

Peas will be ready, and still have a slight crunch under the teeth, after 3–5 minutes; courgettes will take about 3 minutes. When both *primeurs* have cooked, drain the *mange-tout*, add pepper and more salt if need be; season courgettes.

Divide among 4 heated side plates and serve.

Crémant sorbet

Make this 36 hours in advance of dinner, as wine-based mixtures take a long time to freeze.

240 g/8 oz/scant 1¼ cups
   granulated sugar
360 ml/12 fl oz/1½ cups water
10 g/scant ½ oz powdered gelatine,
   or 3 leaves European gelatine

900 ml/1½ pints/1 quart dry, fruity
   méthode champenoise wine,
   well-chilled
Juice of 1½ large lemons
1½ egg whites

Dissolve sugar in the water and boil for 10 minutes while soaking the gelatine in a little more water, or if using leaves, in a water-filled jug. Remove hot syrup from the fire, scoop in the gelatine (drained of water if in leaf form), and dissolve it by swirling the pan. Cool completely.

Combine the syrup, sparkling wine, and strained lemon juice, stir well, and pour into a deep plastic box or metal container. Cover with a lid and place in the freezer. After several hours, when the mixture is semi-frozen, beat the egg whites to peaks, beat them into the sorbet and refreeze. After 2 hours, scrape the sides of the box and thoroughly whisk the ice. Repeat scraping and whisking at intervals during the day to encourage uniformity of texture.

The sorbet will set into a soft crystalline mass. To serve, scoop it into

4 wineglasses that have been frosted in the freezer and bring to the table without delay. As the ice melts on your tongue, the wine bursts into effervescence.

Cœurs à la crème

If you can't find French, white-glazed, hole-pierced, earthenware moulds for this recipe, substitute 9 cm/3½ in heart-shaped cookie cutters set over a close-meshed rack.

240 ml/8 fl oz/1 cup each thick
  cream and plain yoghurt
3 egg whites
Fresh geranium leaves or other
  greenery

Prepare *cœur à la crème* moulds by lining each with a square of cheesecloth or muslin.

Whip the cream until stiff, beat the yoghurt smooth and fold the two together; beat the egg whites to soft peaks and fold all into one.

Spoon the mixture into the 4 moulds until each is slightly too full, rap on the work surface to settle contents, fold the cheesecloth over the cream, and place the moulds on flat plates in the refrigerator or larder to drain overnight. The cream will set into hearts.

To serve, wash and dry whatever leaves you choose and overlap onto 4 small plates. Carefully fold back the cloth from each mould and invert them one by one onto centre of leaves. Lift off the moulds, detach cloths gently, smooth any ragged edges, and serve with a green salad dressed in a very mild version of the vinaigrette on page 221.

Tarte Tatin aux poires

If you're unable to get fresh pears from *somewhere* for this early summer meal, fall back on the ubiquitous apple.

150 g/5 oz/¾ cup granulated sugar   *45 g/1½ oz butter, unsalted if*
3–4 round, medium-sized pears, a   *possible*
  little under-ripe

Another 30 g/2 tbs granulated   *2.5 ml/½ teasp brandy*
*   sugar*   *Shortcrust I, page 222*

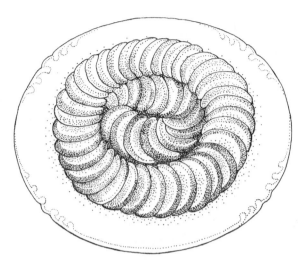

Have ready a clean and dry, straight-sided, round aluminium cake tin measuring 20 × 4 cm/8 in across × 1½ in deep.

Make a caramel by dissolving the first lot of sugar with a little water in a small heavy saucepan. Do this over a low heat with a lid on the saucepan, swirling periodically, and when every grain of sugar has melted, raise the heat and bring the sugar up to a good colour (about 182°C/360°F, or a little higher). Pour this carefully over the bottom of the tin, tilting the tin to cover completely. Cool in the refrigerator until the caramel hardens.

Peel, quarter, and core the pears, slice each quarter lengthwise into 4 equal parts. Melt 15 g/½ oz butter in a heavy sauté pan and toss half the slices, sprinkled with one 15-ml spoon/1 tbs sugar, over a high heat for a minute or two until the fruit is beginning to cook but remains firm inside. Turn onto a cake rack set over a bowl to cool, and drain the fruit thoroughly. Repeat with the remaining pear, sugar, and 15 g/½ oz butter. As pears are a watery fruit, it is important to the success of this dessert that they be well-drained after cooking.

When the caramel is hard and the pears cool, arrange the slices closely overlapping in two alternating circles on the caramel, starting from the tin's outside edge, with the outside edge of each slice against the bottom of the tin. Melt the remaining butter, add the brandy, and pour this over the pears.

Roll out ⅓ of the shortcrust (use the remainder elsewhere), cut a circle that just fits inside the tin and place it over the fruit. Refrigerate for at least an hour; you can prepare things to this point on the morning of your dinner, and bake the tart while eating the duck.

When ready to go, place the tin in the middle of a 220°C/425°F/gas mark 7 oven and bake for 35–40 minutes, looking after 20 minutes to see if the pastry is browning too much; if so, cover it with foil. The crust should be a deep golden-brown and the syrup boiling and heavy round the edges when the tart is ready.

Cool it for 15 minutes in the tin, place the metal round from the bottom of a 2-piece cake pan – or a circle of heavy, foil-wrapped cardboard – on top of the pastry and, with a smart gesture, invert the tart onto a cake rack set over a clean bowl to catch the excess syrup (reserve this). The pears will have absorbed their caramel and turned a dark and mellow gold.

Transfer the tart with its circular support to a flat serving plate, pull away the support, and slice the *Tatin* into small portions. The dessert is rich and sweet, and the one or two who want second helpings can go round again. Spoon the syrup, drained after baking, over each slice and serve warm.

If the baked tart must wait for guests to catch up, keep it warm in the tin and turn it out just before serving.

A menu for sophisticated vegetarians
for six

TOMATO CHUTNEY SORBET

BRINJAL CURRY
RICE AND INDIAN BREAD

A SEASONAL SALAD

FRESH FRUIT

RAVA

A menu for sophisticated vegetarians
for six

Informal but rather stylish, this meal should also tempt the carniverous and is fit for any month of the year.

Bomi Kavarana hails from Bombay, and his 45-minute *brinjal* or aubergine curry is medium hot, copious, and good. Its cost is rock-bottom during the weeks when aubergines are cheap and plentiful, and it set me thinking in an Indian direction. Why not a tomato chutney sorbet beforehand, leading towards the curry's own dash of tomato and mustard? The iced heat of ginger and chili spiced with cinnamon and sweetened by raisins is definitely eccentric, but we – and some guests who were captive tasters – decided we loved it.

After curry and *chapati* a seasonal salad to cool the palate, my favourites the summer purslane and a little later, nasturtiums – both flowers and leaves – with cucumber. Read on!

Fruit follows, and then the most seductive Indian pudding, a Parsi dish from Bombay based on semolina, spices, and rose-water. Contributed by cooking teacher Jenny Kavarana, *rava* has the texture of soft curd cheese; its scented loveliness is persuasive enough to convert even firm opponents of this modest grain.

This is an easy meal to make. The ice and *rava* should be done on the previous day, the curry takes roughly 45 minutes, and the salads are prepared as you eat them.

AWS

We've avoided the temptation to suggest carrot, potato or dandelion wine, though in the hands of a talented olitorian – our coined word for a *vigneron* who works with vegetables, not grapes – they can be good.

Nor, because of its peculiar flavour, do we recommend the sage-scented vermouth of Provence. If the season is right and you want to keep within the vegetable idiom, a Pimm's cup, with its borage and cucumber, might serve as aperitif, though the assertive flavour of chutney ice will quickly despatch its memory.

Curry doesn't flatter any wine, but many people like it with a fruity white or rosé. Bomi suggests cold lager beer, cider, "or just water"; we recommend that "just water" be sparkling and the cider a gentle, *pétillant* Norman-style rather than a strong English one. Alternatively, one of the excellent mild apple wines or juices now on the market.

The fruits and *rava* are a matter for the whole spectrum of rich white or golden wines that are their excellent complements. Try the Greek mavrodaphne – for a change; or a 3-*puttonos* tokay from Hungary, a liqueur Muscat de Beaumes de Venise from the Rhône Valley in France – or one of its sweet cousins from Samos (Greece), Setúbal (Portugal), Victoria (Australia) or Worcester (South Africa). A truly cosmopolitan family!

HD-M

Tomato chutney sorbet

This makes enough for 8 and is finished with a dash of gin.

800 g/1 lb 10 oz of canned
   tomatoes and their juices
60 ml/4 tbs cider or wine vinegar
180 g/6 oz chopped onions
2 cloves chopped garlic
Two 5-ml spoons/2 teasp grated
   fresh ginger root
120 g/4 oz chopped apple
120 g/4 oz/⅔ cup light brown sugar
A seeded and minced fresh chili
1 stick cinnamon

A handful of fresh coriander, roots
   off, stems and leaves
   finely-chopped
One 5-ml spoon/1 teasp salt
One 15-ml spoon/1 tbs
   concentrated tomato paste
Five 15-ml spoons/5 tbs raisins
Two 15-ml spoons/2 tbs each olive
   oil and black mustard seeds
2 egg whites
Dash gin
Cheese straws

Put the first eleven ingredients into a saucepan, bring them to the boil and simmer for 25 minutes, adding the tomato paste for the last 5 minutes of cooking.

Meanwhile, coarsely chop the raisins and plump them in some just-boiled water.

Let the chutney cool a bit, remove the cinnamon and purée the mixture in the food processor, leaving it with a certain amount of texture. Remove to a bowl, drain the raisins well, and add them to the mix. Cool.

Heat the olive oil in a small saucepan, add the mustard seeds and warm them till they jump. Set a lid on the pan, remove it from the heat, and pour both seeds and oil into the chutney. Stir well, turn into a deep plastic box or metal container, put a lid on, and freeze until the chutney is firm but still slightly slushy.

Whisk the egg whites to peaks, turn the sorbet into the food processor and whiz it a few times to a soft and fluffy consistency. Turn into a bowl, fold in the egg whites – with a good dash of gin – and refreeze. It becomes very hard.

Make this 24 hours ahead of serving, and transfer it to the refrigerator an hour before scooping into frosted glasses. Serve with cheese straws, home-made if possible.

Brinjal curry

Ghee – sold in tins – is a kind of clarified butter that melts to a clear golden liquid with a high burning point. Vegetable oil may be used instead, but is not as authentic. This recipe makes enough for 6 and a little over.

240 g/8 oz vegetable ghee
1 kg/2¼ lbs large onions
1 heaped 5-ml spoon/1 heaped teasp whole cloves
Salt
1½ kg/3¼ lb brinjals or aubergines (egg-plants)
One 15-ml spoon/1 tbs each black mustard seeds, cumin seeds, and ground turmeric

1 heaped 15-ml spoon/1 heaped tbs Kashmiri masala, or a hot and rich curry paste
1 heaped 15-ml spoon/1 heaped tbs granulated sugar
150 g/5 oz concentrated tomato paste

Melt all but 15 g/½ oz of the ghee in two large sauté pans, peel and chop the onions very fine and fry them until brownish. Stir periodically to prevent burning, and add the cloves about half way through cooking.

Bring a large pot of salted water to the boil, cut the unpeeled aubergines into 2 cm/¾ in cubes and boil them for about 5 minutes or until nearly cooked. Drain the aubergines and retain their water.

Heat the remaining ghee in a small saucepan, add the black mustard seeds and – as for the chutney sorbet – warm them until they begin to crackle and pop. Clap a lid on the pan and remove it from the heat. Put the seeds and ghee with the onions, followed by cumin, turmeric, Kashmiri masala or hot curry paste, sugar, a 5-ml spoon/1 teasp of salt, and tomato paste. Stir thoroughly. Drop in the cubed aubergines and simmer for about 10 minutes, adding enough of the cooking water to give the curry a somewhat wet consistency.

Serve with boiled basmati rice and Indian breads like paratha, roti, nan, or chapati.

Dr. Bomi J. Kavarana, Mid-Surrey Wine & Food Society, England

A seasonal salad

As a contrast to curry, a salad of seasonal leaves dressed lightly with olive oil, a dash of lemon, some salt and pepper and a touch of French mustard. Or in spring, for the lucky few, a salad of the pink petals of quince flowers, without dressing.

In winter and spring, a bowl of the slightly nut-flavoured lamb's lettuce, also known as corn salad and to the French as *mâche*, or the leaves of red chicory; in summer the rare and succulent purslane – *pourpier* in French – one of the nicest salads there is and worth searching for; in early summer and autumn the deep-cut, peppery leaves of rocket or arugula, perhaps combined with any lettuce but iceberg.

But the best of all salads can be made in late summer and early autumn if you grow nasturtiums – and some lucky people have gardens packed with them. Pick, stem, wash, and dry handfuls of nasturtium leaves, slice peeled or unpeeled cucumbers very thin, snip chives, and toss the elements with a little dressing. Scatter on orange or scarlet nasturtium flowers. The pungent leaves and the crunch of ingredients are a striking and delicious combination.

Rava

A pinch of saffron threads
60–75 ml/4–5 tbs rose-water – for cooking, not perfumery
24 green or white cardamom pods
120 g/4 oz semolina – not pre-cooked or quick-cooking varieties
90 g/3 oz butter, unsalted if possible

1200 ml/2 pints/5 cups milk
120 g/4 oz/scant ⅔ cup castor (granulated) sugar
60 g/2 oz ground almonds
Grated nutmeg
90 g/3 oz whole almonds in their skins
60 g/2 oz dried currants

Put the threads of saffron into a warm place to dry out, and when they are crisp, crumble to a fine powder between the thumb and forefinger. Drop the powder into a small heat-proof bowl, bring the rose-water to a boil and pour it over the saffron. Leave to infuse for 10 minutes, which draws out the saffron's colour and flavour.

Remove seeds from the cardamom pods and discard the husks. Place the seeds and semolina in the container of an electric grinder and grind for several seconds or until the seeds break up. They may not reduce to a complete powder; it doesn't matter.

Melt the butter in a large, heavy saucepan and add the semolina and cardamom. Stirring constantly to avoid browning, cook for a minute or two over moderate heat. Remove from the fire and gradually add the milk, stirring well between pours. When all the milk has been incorporated, return the pan to the heat and, stirring, bring the semolina to the boil. Add the rose-water mixture, the sugar, and the ground almonds. Let the pudding cook gently, stirring occasionally, until it thickens and leaves a thin trail when dribbled from a spoon. Pour this into a large glass serving bowl. Grate the nutmeg lightly and evenly over the *rava*, allow it to cool, and chill overnight.

A few hours before serving, blanch the almonds for a minute in boiling water and remove their skins. Shred them into fine sticks and grill or broil these until golden-brown. Mix nuts with the currants, and just before serving, strew the top of the pudding – about half an hour out of the refrigerator – with this combination, added at the last minute to prevent the *rava*'s moisture from softening the nuts.

Jenny Kavarana, Surrey, England

A good excuse for chicken

for six

SALMON AND SCALLOP MOUSSE,
HOLLANDAISE SAUCE WITH DILL

RED PEPPER CHICKEN
BUTTERED NOODLES

MELON BISCUITS WITH SLICED FRESH MELON

A good excuse for chicken
for six

These menus do not lack chicken – all of it fairly exotic – but cookery book author Rachel Norman's poultry with sweet red and hot chili peppers is our certain favourite. The chili-warmth pervades both bird and sauce, and the red pepper-sweetness restrains the fire. The result is delicious and unusual, the ingredients more bounty from the kitchen gardener of page 26. With this, plenty of boiled, buttered noodles to absorb the flavours.

Before the deep terracotta colours of the chicken, a rich ring of fish mousse from Harriet and Bill Lembeck, who run the Beverage Program of wine courses at the Waldorf-Astoria Hotel in New York. Fresh salmon modifies the intensity of smoked, and sea scallops bring both sweetness and the liaison of their natural gelatine to that of the salmon. Add a dill-laced hollandaise and settle well into the heart of summer!

Melon "biscuits" is a fanciful name for very light melon custards, flavoured with honey and dessert wine and served with fans of chilled melon and a dash more drink. Do choose the most aromatic and flavourful melons you can find for both biscuits and fans, or the result will be bland.

Biscuits are done in the morning, or the night before, as is most preparation for the chicken; the mousse is put together early and simply baked to serve, and even the hollandaise can be held for an hour after making. So the cook is not lost to the guests.

AWS

The Lembecks sent us this mousse, they say, in honour of Alice! To return the compliment, I propose as accompaniment a bottle-fermented sparkling wine from New York State like Bully Hill or Great Western Gold Seal, whose winery, as Harriet points out in her splendid edition of *Grossman's Guide to Wines, Beers, and Spirits*, was winning prizes in *France* as far back as 1867. Sparklers of excellent quality, made by the *méthode champenoise*, also come from Spain and Italy. Readers without access to any of these will find that the French produce acceptable substitutes!

Red pepper chicken calls for one of the world's distinctive "hot" wines. If, therefore, you can find a red Château Musar from the Lebanon, the deep crimson Mascara of Algeria, or Morocco's special rosé, the Gris de Boulouanne, you can arrange an interesting marriage. South Africans and Australians might try one of their shiraz-based bottles.

Wine for melon is a long-standing problem. Indeed, Christophers, wine merchants in London since the 17th century, once held a competition to find the ideal wine to accompany this luscious fruit. The prizewinner suggested coteaux de layon from the Loire, but in those days the Rhône wine Muscat de Beaumes de Venise was unknown in England. This, or any of the other sweet muscats mentioned on page 71, would be my choice, and it would be logical to use the same one in baking the "biscuits".

HD-M

Salmon and scallop mousse

Butter

120 g/4 oz fresh salmon, weighed after skinning and boning

120 g/4 oz each smoked salmon and bay or sea scallops, fresh if possible

1 white of a large egg

240 ml/8 fl oz/1 cup thick cream

One 2.5-ml spoon/$\frac{1}{2}$ teasp chopped fresh dill

Salt and pepper

Copiously butter an 18 cm/7 in savarin or ring mould.

Cut up all the fish and purée it, with the egg white, in the food processor until the mixture is very smooth. Transfer to a bowl set into a larger, ice-lined container, and gradually beat cream into the fish base. Add the chopped dill, season well with salt (remembering that smoked salmon is salty) and pepper. Pile this into the savarin mould, rap the mould on the work surface to settle its contents, wet your hand and smooth over the top. Cover the fish with a well-buttered circle of greaseproof or parchment paper with a hole in the centre to allow for the escape of steam, and refrigerate. You can make this in the morning and let it rest until evening, if convenient; if making later, rest the mousse, moulded and refrigerated, for at least an hour before proceeding.

Set the mould on a wire rack inside an ovenproof container, add simmering water to come half way up the sides and bake at 165°C/325°F/gas mark 3 for about 25 minutes, or until the mousse feels springy to your touch.

Remove the mould from its *bain-marie* and let it rest in a warm place for 10 minutes. Peel away the paper and turn the mould over onto a rack set above a plate or bowl to catch any juices that will drain away. Leave for a minute, turn the fish right side up again and unmould onto a serving plate. Hand round hollandaise sauce, made as described below.

Harriet and William Lembeck, New York Wine & Food Society, USA

Hollandaise sauce with dill

30 ml/2 tbs each dry white wine
    and water
Lemon juice
4 egg yolks

180–240 g/6–8 oz cold butter,
    preferably unsalted
Salt and pepper
Fresh dill

In a small heavy saucepan reduce the wine and water to 15 ml/1 tbs, squeeze in a few drops of lemon juice and let the liquid cool for a moment. Add the egg yolks, whisk them, and have to hand the butter, cut into 30 g/1 oz cubes.

If you are an accomplished maker of egg-based sauces you can probably proceed with this one over a direct fire; otherwise heat a shallow pan of water to just below the simmer, put the yolk-pan inside and whisk the contents – watching like a hawk for signs of scrambling – to a thickened foam, like a light custard that forms soft peaks when you lift the whisk.

Remove yolks from the heat and beat in a piece of cold butter; as it is absorbed, gradually whisk in more butter until at least 180 g/6 oz have been used and a frothy sauce appears that lightly coats a spoon's back. Season with lemon juice, salt and pepper, add a little chopped dill to taste, and serve in a slightly warmed sauce boat.

You can hold this hollandaise in its pan for up to an hour, set in a container of hottish water. Stir gently before transferring to the boat to serve.

Red pepper chicken

Red "bell" peppers – as they say in America – are subtler than green ones so preferable here. This will serve 8 – or 6 with two extra helpings.

2 fresh, oven-ready chickens,
   about 1400 g/3 lb each, dressed
   weight
6 sweet red peppers; green will
   substitute if necessary
2 fresh chili peppers
2 large onions
8 cloves garlic
6 large fresh tomatoes, or a
   sizeable can of plum tomatoes
480 g/1 lb mushrooms
A large handful each of fresh
   parsley and basil

60 ml/4 tbs olive oil
60 g/2 oz butter
Salt
360 ml/12 fl oz/1½ cups dry white
   wine, plus more at the end
360 ml/12 fl oz/1½ cups chicken
   broth (see recipe)
One 15-ml spoon/1 tbs cornflour
   (cornstarch)
Boiled, buttered noodles, fresh if
   possible

Cut the chickens into a total of 8 serving pieces, and use the carcasses and appropriate giblets to make the chicken broth needed for this recipe, following the method set out on page 219.

Remove skins of the sweet peppers by turning them under a grill (broiler) until the skins blister and blacken. Cool under wet kitchen paper to trap the steam that helps loosen these, peel them away, open the peppers, remove and discard all seeds, and cut the flesh into short, narrow strips.

Cut open the chilis, remove their seeds and finely sliver the flesh. Peel and thinly slice the onions, peel and slightly crush the garlic. Peel, seed, and chop the fresh tomatoes; or, if using canned ones, drain them of juice and chop them roughly. Quarter and wash the mushrooms, chop half the parsley, and scissor half the basil leaves into narrow strips.

Heat a very large, heavy casserole – or two smaller ones – put in half the oil and butter, and sauté the chilis, onion and garlic until they are lightly browned. Remove with a slotted spoon. Add the remaining oil and butter and brown the chicken pieces on both sides. Remove them, wipe away their excess oil, and pour the remaining oil and butter out of the casserole(s).

Return the dark meat and sautéed vegetables to the casseroles, pour in the wine, and for two minutes, simmer away some of the alcohol. Add the sliced sweet peppers, tomatoes, mushrooms, the chopped/ scissored parsley and basil, and salt. Pour on the chicken broth. All this can be done in advance, if you wish, and the dish then finished just before serving.

Cover the casseroles, bring the liquid to a boil, and simmer over a very low heat for 30–35 minutes, adding the white chicken, which takes less time to cook, 15 minutes after the rest, and basting the meat with its juices from time to time. (Cooking will probably take a little longer if the dish has been refrigerated after preliminaries).

Meanwhile, chop and shred the remaining parsley and basil. When the chicken tests done, remove it – with as many pepper strips as is feasible – to a hot platter, cover it with a little of the cooking liquid, put foil on top, and hold the platter at the bottom of a low oven while finishing the sauce.

Combine all the juices in one casserole, skim them of fat – spooning this carefully away – raise the heat and reduce the juices to about half. Refresh the flavour with a few drops of white wine. Dissolve the cornflour (cornstarch) in $1\frac{1}{2}$ × 15-ml spoons/$1\frac{1}{2}$ tbs water, and stir in about a 15-ml spoon/1 tbs of this; let the sauce bubble and simmer and thicken slightly, then judge whether to add the remaining cornflour. The result should not be thicker than the consisistency that barely coats the back of a spoon.

Check the seasoning – ground pepper should not be necessary – and serve the chicken on a bed of noodles, some of the sauce poured on, the herbs sprinkled over and the rest of the sauce passed in a warm boat.

Rachel H. Norman, Marin County Wine & Food Society, California, USA

Melon biscuits with sliced fresh melon

420 g/14 oz flesh of ripe, aromatic summer melon like gallia, ogen, charentais (cavaillon), or cantaloup
150 ml/5 fl oz/scant ⅔ cup Muscat de Beaumes de Venise, or other

sweet muscat wine, plus more at the end
About 30 ml/2 tbs runny honey
30 ml/2 tbs lemon juice
4 eggs

2 or 3 extra melons of the same
   variety and ripeness, well-chilled
   (see recipe)

Fresh mint and more muscat as
   garnish

Purée the melon flesh in the blender or food processor until completely
smooth, while reducing the 150 ml/5 fl oz/⅔ cup of Muscat de Beaumes
de Venise, over a brisk heat, to the value of 15 ml/1 tbs. Add this to the
melon purée with the honey and lemon juice and blend. Whisk in the
eggs and add a quick pour of muscat to sharpen the flavour.

Butter 6 heatproof ramekins of 150 ml/5 fl oz/scant ⅔ cup capacity,
line the bottom of each with a buttered circle of greaseproof or
parchment paper, and bake the custards in a *bain-marie* in the middle of
a 155°C/310°F/gas mark 2 oven for 60–90 minutes, or until they are firm
and risen.

Remove the ramekins from their *bain-marie* and cool them on a wire
rack. When cool, refrigerate for at least 8 hours or overnight.

To serve, cut the extra melons into six 180 g/6 oz wedges, remove the
rind, and cut each wedge thinly along its length into 4 or 5 slices. Fan
each set of slices across individual plates, unmould each biscuit into the
spring of the fan, peel off the paper, dash a bit of muscat over the top,
garnish with a small sprig of mint and serve.

Late supper, wild mushrooms
for four

BLACK BEAN SOUP

WILD MUSHROOM TOASTS

CLARET SORBET
VINE LEAF SHORTBREADS

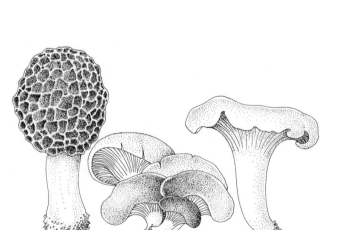

Late supper, wild mushrooms
for four

A recommendation for chilly nights and warming supper after theatre or cinema. Morels, fairy ring mushrooms, and a few ceps shoot up in the spring, but most of the world's best wild species are late summer growths which disappear with the hard frosts, so aim this supper for the early autumn.

First, a good, thick, and stalwart Southern American black bean soup of slightly smoky flavour. We asked John Bruno, owner of New York's Pen and Pencil Restaurant, the difference between black "turtle" beans – specified in his recipe – and the kidney-shaped variety we buy in England. He immediately air-mailed us a large bag of "Number One Grade Black Turtle Beans"; we liked this gesture! They proved to be smaller versions of the dried ones we know, and both types make successful soup.

Last October we went mushrooming for the first time, near London, under the tutelage of two Italian chefs, both of whom have mushroomed yearly since they were small boys in Lombardy. The Surrey wood of birches and chestnuts was sunny, still, and cold after heavy rains of the previous week. These, following an overly dry summer, meant a poor season for mushrooms, said the brothers Pertusini (ideal conditions being a warm summer with *some* rain, and a mild autumn), but still we – or rather they – found about two kilos of various types of cep or *Boletus edulis*. Two kilos for a morning's work was a meagre haul, they asserted, but we were thrilled. Wild mushroom soup and the jiffy toasts polished off the booty – of excellent flavour and not waterlogged – in two days.

An alternative to the wild toasts would be Len Evans' tame

mushrooms with kidneys and leeks on page 205, but in either case, end the supper lightly with a glassful of claret sorbet and shortbreads cut in the shape of vine leaves.

This is an ideal meal for quick production on a late evening. The soup has been made and need only be reheated, the mushrooms and trimmings can be cleaned and readied before you go out and quickly cooked while you brown the toast; the sorbet and shortbreads are set to be served.

AWS

Why not a meal like this after tasting wine? Personally, I find all that spitting tones up the appetite.

It's often said that the red wines of Tuscany are perfumed like mushrooms, so let's open a bottle of chianti, or one of the newer Florentine alternatives – such as Tignanello or Sassicaia, both of which age well, or the lesser-known Carmignano. These are wines which temper the sangiovese grape with the finesse of cabernet sauvignon. Most wine-making countries outside Europe produce something in the style of northern Italy, so there should be no problems (unless you live in Germany – or England!) about choosing a domestic alternative. If French wines are all you can lay hands on, we suggest a red of the Loire – a bourgueil or perhaps a chinon.

Any one of these should see you through the meal, and the sorbet hardly requires drink, but if you think John Bruno's enigmatic black bean soup deserves a bottle to itself, we wouldn't argue. How about a lightly-chilled Rhine wine or an Alsatian gewürztraminer, or one of their interesting imitators from the southern hemisphere?

HD-M

Black bean soup

This recipe, for 4, will feed 6 people of smaller appetites.

360 g/12 oz black beans, turtle or
  otherwise
60 g/2 oz each pork and veal
One 120 g/4 oz onion
1 large clove garlic
1 stalk celery
One 1.25-ml spoon/¼ teasp dried
  basil

1 small bay leaf
1200 ml/2 pints/5 cups meat broth
  (page 220)
Salt and pepper
Juice of ½ a large lemon
A few slices of boiled ham
Thick cream

Wash the beans, put them into a large pot, and cover with copious water to soak overnight. The next day, bring the water to a boil and boil the beans hard – without salt – for 20 minutes or until quite tender. Drain the beans, reserving their cooking liquid, and roughly purée them.

Meanwhile, cube the meats, peel and slice the onion, peel and crush the garlic, cut up the celery and put this, with the herbs, into another pot with 900 ml/1½ pints/4 cups of the meat broth, add a pinch of salt, bring to the boil and simmer for 50 minutes, or till the meat is cooked. Drain meat and vegetables, hold the broth, remove the bay leaf, and roughly purée the rest.

Return the bean purée to the large pot with both lots of meat broth, add 600 ml/1 pint/2½ cups of the beans' cooking liquid and simmer for 1 hour. Add the puréed meat, salt and pepper to taste, and rub the soup through a coarse sieve. Add the strained juice of the half-lemon and more bean stock if necessary to thin the result.

When ready to serve, reheat the soup, ladle it into bowls, and top each with some shredded ham and a small swirl of thick cream.

John Charles Bruno, New York Wine & Food Society, USA

Wild mushroom toasts

Only the rich, silky flavours of fresh wild mushrooms will do to make this an exceptional little dish. We've tried it with both ceps and chanterelles (*Cantharellus cibarius*) and could eat it often.

720 g/1½ lb, pared weight, wild   *Olive oil*
     mushrooms: ceps, morels, oyster   *An infused wine vinegar:*
     mushrooms, horns of plenty,   *elderflower, tarragon,*
     chanterelles, or whatever   *strawberry, nasturtium, clove,*
2 large cloves garlic   *or some such other*
3 or 4 shallots   *4 pieces of buttered whole meal or*
A handful of fresh parsley   *whole wheat toast*

If using ceps, pare the stem ends, inspect the stems for worm damage and pare or discard any badly affected or decaying bits. Wipe the ceps well with a damp cloth and cut them into largish pieces. Trim, wash, and thoroughly drain other mushrooms and cut them up if necessary –

wild mushrooms shrink a lot in cooking, so don't make the pieces too small.

Peel and mince garlic and shallots, finely chop the parsley. All this can be done ahead of need, covered with a damp cloth, and refrigerated.

Run a light film of oil over one or two large heavy sauté pans, heat the oil, salt the mushrooms and toss them over a fairly high heat. All the fungi will give off liquid which is then reabsorbed and evaporated – except in the case of chanterelles, whose expelled juices must be drained away (and can be used in soup) – as they come to the boil. So drain the latter, return them to the pan with a little more oil, and proceed with the recipe.

As the mushrooms are in the midst of cooking, make the toast, butter it, and keep it warm on four hot plates.

After 5 – 7 – 10 minutes – when mushrooms are tender, have dried, and begun to colour – add the garlic, shallots, and parsley, toss, add a good splash of vinegar. Let this bubble away – there will be an explosion of aromas – grind on salt and pepper, toss again, fling the mushrooms onto their toasts and serve immediately.

Claret sorbet

The proportions and technique for this sorbet are the same as for the *crémant* palate cleanser on page 65 but the "ice" here is slotted into use as a light chaser of a filling meal. Like the *crémant*, make it 36 hours ahead of serving. Alternatives to claret are listed below, and vine leaf shortbreads are an amusing extra.

240 g/8 oz/scant 1¼ cups granulated sugar
360 ml/12 fl oz/1½ cups water
10 g/scant ½ oz powdered gelatine, or 3 leaves European gelatine
900 ml/1½ pints/1 quart good inexpensive claret, or a light red cabernet from California or
Australia, or a shiraz, none more than five years old, well-chilled
Juice of 1½ large lemons
1½ egg whites
Black grapes, if available, as garnish

Dissolve sugar in the water and boil for 10 minutes while soaking the gelatine in a little more water, or if using leaves, in a water-filled jug.

Remove the hot syrup from the fire, scoop in the gelatine (drained of water if in leaf form), and dissolve it by swirling the syrup's pan. Cool completely.

Combine the syrup, wine, and strained lemon juice, stir well, and pour into a deep plastic box or metal container. Cover with a lid and place in the freezer. After several hours, when the mixture is semi-frozen, beat the egg whites to peaks, beat them into the sorbet and refreeze. After 2 hours, scrape sides of the box and thoroughly whisk the ice. Repeat scraping and whisking at intervals during the day to encourage uniformity of texture.

When set, the sorbet will be a rather soft crystalline mass. Scoop it into "grapes" with a melon baller and fill 4 tall wine glasses that have been frosted in the freezer. Serve without delay – alcohol-based sorbets melt quickly – on dessert plates garnished with small bunches of black grapes, and pass round the vine leaf shortbreads.

Vine leaf shortbreads

Makes about 20–25 leaves.

120 g/4 oz butter, softened and
  preferably unsalted
150 g/5 oz/¾ cup castor
  (granulated) sugar
1 egg
About 30 ml/ 2 tbs milk

360 g/12 oz/a scant 2½ cups plain
  flour
A large pinch of salt
One 5-ml spoon/1 teasp baking
  powder

Cream the butter until light, and gradually add the sugar. Whisk the egg to break it up and beat it into the butter in two pours. Beat in 30 ml/2 tbs of milk.

Sift together the dry ingredients and work them into the mixture until it comes together. The dough should be moist but not damp – if necessary, add a few drops more milk to achieve this. Roll into a ball, wrap the ball in greaseproof or waxed paper and refrigerate until firm but not hard.

Break off bits of the dough and roll them out on a floured board to the thickness of ½ cm/⅛ in. Using drawings of vine leaves as an inspiration, cut free-hand leaf shapes – about 10 × 10 cm/4 × 4 in – with a small, sharp knife. At first it may seem difficult to get a good likeness, but persevere.

Place the leaves on heavy, lightly-buttered baking sheets and bake at 180°C/350°F/gas mark 4 for about 10 minutes, or until the edges are golden-brown. Cool on the sheets for a minute or two before removing leaves with a spatula to cake racks. When cold, store them carefully – they're rather fragile – in airtight tins, where they will keep for weeks.

A grand autumn dinner
for six

COQUILLES ST-JACQUES EN FEUILLETÉS
Scallops in puff pastry shells

or

CONSOMMÉ DE BŒUF
Beef consommé

BŒUF À LA FICELLE
Fillet of beef on-a-string

SOUFFLÉ GLACÉ AUX CANNEBERGES
Iced cranberry soufflé

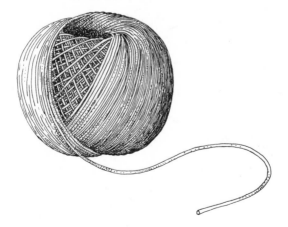

A grand autumn dinner
for six

Bœuf à la ficelle is a famous old dish that one hardly sees now in public or private – partly due, I'm sure, to the price of beef fillet, but also I suspect because private cooks are alarmed by the notion of poaching such a cut in large amounts of beef broth. But take a chance – the result is quite wonderful: rare and tender and filled with flavour, accompanied by its many vegetables and condiments.

The only thing grand about this festive *plat* is the meat's current price; tradition has it that nineteenth-century workers at the Paris abattoirs found the fillet an easy cut to remove discreetly from beast and premises. When they reached the *bistro*, out came the fillet, round went a string, and down dropped the meat into a pot of whatever was simmering at the time – often the ubiquitous *pot-au-feu*. The string was tied to the pot's handle so that the fillet (or fillets) could be hauled out conveniently, and *voilà* dinner.

I first tasted this in the minute Paris restaurant of Madame Marie-Antoinette Cartet, an inspired cook (now retired) from the Ain, east of Lyon, and a woman in the great tradition of Lyon's female chefs like la Mère Fillioux and la Mère Brazier. Each bite of Madame Cartet's *bœuf ficelle*, served with a wine and shallot sauce, literally seemed to vanish on the tongue.

Before the beef, quite a glamorous helping of vermouth-poached scallops in puff pastry cases and a cream and butter sauce. Try, if possible, to get the scallops in their shells, proof that the seafood have not been frozen; the fishmonger will clean them for you, and be sure he gives back the coral or roe – not often seen, we gather, in America, where the recipe comes from. If this sounds too rich for you, serve

94

instead the broth of the *bœuf* as a sort of informal *consommé*. To do this, poach the beef, keep back sufficient broth in which to heat its accompanying vegetables, pour the remainder through a muslin-lined sieve, and while the fillet is resting, serve the broth in soup bowls floated with garlic-rubbed slices of French bread dried out in a low oven.

The *soufflé glacé* from Lyn Hall rises high above its dish – supported while freezing by a paper collar – and rouses approving cries when brought to the table. North of the equator, fresh cranberries are available in October and November, and the spice and tart sparkle of this dessert, topped with cranberries simmered in wine and cider, have convinced me that the cranberry sauces of my childhood Thanksgivings were only a beginning!

Elements of the *coquilles* and beef, plus vegetables, can be prepared well ahead, but both fish and meat must be finished at the last minute; the soufflé is made on the day before, and its topping simmered a few hours in advance of dinner.

AWS

Nancy Minor-Denni proposes a "big full-bodied French or Californian chardonnay" with the *coquilles St-Jacques*, and who are we to argue? If French is elected, we feel the recipe justifies a *premier cru* chablis; if American, a mature Sonoma. The same grape flourishes in Australia's Hunter Valley, and in New Zealand, Cook's offer a good bottling. In South Africa, where one eats wonderful seafood, I would look for a crisp steen from Cape Province.

If you decide on the *consommé*, however, it's a chance to serve an old dry oloroso sherry; wines in this style are available in every country.

The beef-on-a-string may have started humbly, but it ain't humble now. Even beef Wellington was reputedly devised by an army cook to keep the Old Warrior going on the battlefield, and we find a special affinity between good beef and the cabernet sauvignon grape. So we would choose a red wine of Bordeaux or one of its cousins from Australia, the Napa Valley of California, or Italy.

The sweet is luscious and worthy of a German *auslëse*, a sweet bonnezeaux from the Loire or one of the late-harvested rieslings of California or South Africa. If you brought back a bottle of Radgona Tigermilk from Yugoslavia, it would rise to the occasion.

HD-M

Coquilles St-Jacques en feuilletés

960 g/2 lb puff pastry (page 223)   480 g/1 lb fresh bay or sea
1 egg yolk   scallops, with coral if possible
2 medium carrots   2 shallots
1 large celery heart   120 ml/4 fl oz/½ cup each dry
2 medium leeks, white part only   white vermouth and thick cream
Salt and pepper   Watercress as garnish
75 g/2¼ oz butter, preferably
    unsalted

First make the puff pastry cases, known in French as *bouchées*. Take up
the amount of puff that you need, give it two more turns, rest it if
necessary, then roll into a manageable rectangle. Cut this in half and
refrigerate one piece. Roll the remaining half to a thickness of ¾ cm/¼ in,
and with a 9 cm/3½ in circular cutter, stamp out 6 evenly-spaced disks.
Use a 5 cm/2 in cutter to remove circles from the centres of 3 disks,
resulting in 3 rings.

Rinse a heavy baking sheet with cold water, give it a shake, and
invert the 3 intact disks on the sheet at 1½ cm/½ in intervals. Brush the
tops of the disks with cold water and press a ring of pastry onto each.
Lightly press together the layers of dough as you make closely-spaced
vertical indentations round their circumference with the back of a small
knife, and pierce each pastry ring 4 times with a trussing needle to
encourage even rising.

Thoroughly prick the exposed centre of each disk with a fork, and
press the 5 cm/2 in cutter into the centres to a depth of ¼ cm/1/16 in; this
will enable a section to be cut out for use as a lid after baking.

Repeat the process with the remaining pastry, making 3 more
bouchées, and put all 6 of them into the refrigerator for 30 minutes to
relax the dough. Use the pastry off-cuts for something else.

Make a wash by beating the egg yolk with a little water and brush this
over the top of each *bouchée*, carefully avoiding the sides. Score tops
with a knife and bake in a 205°C/400°F/gas mark 6 for 30–35 minutes,
or till well-risen and brown with crisp brown sides. Transfer to a rack,
and with a small knife cut out the lids with a deft sawing motion. Use a
teaspoon to scrape any uncooked pastry from underneath. Let the cases
cool. Use these on the same day, or if making them ahead of time, wrap
well and freeze.

For the *coquilles* filling, peel and trim the carrots and celery heart, wash the leeks well, cut all three into short julienne (matchstick) strips. Melt 15 g/½ oz of the butter in a sauté pan, add the julienne, a little salt, and cover with a lid. Steam slowly for 8–10 minutes or so until tender but still a bit crisp. Add pepper, and more salt if necessary.

If the scallops are large, slice them into 2 or 3 horizontal pieces, retaining their disk-like shape. If they're small, leave them whole, like the coral. Finely chop the shallots and combine them in a saucepan with the vermouth and a pinch of salt. Add the scallops and coral and bring to a simmer; poach the fish very gently for no more than 2–3 minutes until *just* cooked. They must not boil or poach too long or they will certainly toughen.

Remove scallops and keep them hot in a little cooking liquid while reducing the rest by half. At the same time, revive the *bouchées*, whether frozen or not, by placing them on a baking sheet in the centre of a 220°C/425°F/gas mark 7 oven. Turn off the oven and remove pastries, warm and crisp, after 6–8 minutes.

Meanwhile, add the cream to the reduced liquid and let it boil for about 5 minutes, until cream has thickened to a good consistency. Over a low heat, whisk in the 60 g/2 oz of remaining butter, 15 g/½ oz at a time, season, give a final whisk or two, and add vegetables and well-drained scallops. Mix well.

Fill the heated pastry shells, garnish them with their lids and a small bouquet of watercress and serve.

Nancy Minor-Denni, South Bay Wine & Food Society, California, USA

Bœuf à la ficelle

960 g/2 lb assorted beef and veal bones with meat left on them, a piece of shin (fore shank) of mature beef, plus 2 marrow bones, chopped into manageable pieces
Parsley stalks
Bay leaf
4 cloves garlic
One 2.5-ml spoon/½ teasp salt
6 peppercorns

480 g/1 lb each carrots and small turnips
2 fennel bulbs
4 small ripe tomatoes
720 g/1½ lb boiling potatoes
1 "heart of fillet" (tenderloin) of well-aged beef, weighing 1600 g/3½ lb; or up to the whole fillet if necessary to achieve this weight
6 smallish onions, peeled and stuck with 2 cloves each

Garnish

Coarse salt, French mustard –   cucumbers or gherkins which the
   Dijon if possible – and, if   French call cornichons
   available, the small pickled

Put the bones and shank or shin into a very large pot, cover them well
with water, and bring this slowly to the boil. Skim thoroughly and add
the parsley stalks, bay leaf, and unpeeled garlic cloves. Skim again as
the water returns to the boil, add the salt, lower the heat, and simmer
with the lid ajar for about 4 hours, adding peppercorns during the last 20
minutes. Strain the resulting bouillon and top it up with water if
necessary to give the flavour of a good broth. You would have about $2\frac{1}{4}$
litres/4 pints/$2\frac{1}{2}$ quarts.

Meanwhile, peel the carrots and cut them across in half, if long. Slice
them lengthwise into $\frac{3}{4}$ cm/$\frac{1}{4}$ in strips, and do the same for the turnips.
Clean and quarter the fennel bulbs; skin, halve, and peel the tomatoes,
cut the halves in half, and cut the potatoes into 5 cm/2 in olive shapes.
Hold all of these, except the tomatoes, in separate bowls of cold water.

Prepare the beef fillet by removing the loose fat and the muscle
membrane where it covers the flesh. Don't sever the two "chains" of
meat attached to the large muscle. Turn the cleaned fillet so that the
smooth side is uppermost, and if the tail is attached, fold it under the
main part so that the fillet has the same diameter throughout its length.
Tie loops of soft white butchers' string at 3 cm/$1\frac{1}{4}$ in intervals along the
fillet's length, tie the ends, and leave a long loop at one extremity.

Shortly before your guests arrive, remove most of the fat from the top
of the bouillon, bring it to the simmering point, and poach each
vegetable in turn – including onions but excluding potatoes – until just
cooked. Drain and hold them wrapped carefully and separately in damp
kitchen paper.

Just before the meal begins, bring the bouillon to the simmering
point and immerse the potatoes in a saucepan of salted water.

As you sit down for the first course, bring the potatoes to the simmer;
they will cook in 15–20 minutes. Put 2 large platters to heat in a low
oven, lower the fillet into the simmering bouillon and secure the loop to
the pot handle for easy removal. Boil the meat for a few minutes, reduce
the heat, and simmer it for 20 minutes more. The result will be very
rare.

For the final launch, remove the meat from its bouillon and let rest
for 10 minutes; extinguish the fire under the potatoes when these have
cooked. Reheat other vegetables in the bouillon, carve enough thick
slices of meat for 6 people, and arrange them on one of the platters.

Drain the vegetables, halve the onions and arrange a few of each sort around the fillet.

Put remaining vegetables on the second platter with the drained potatoes, cover each platter with a wet and wrung-out tea-towel and heat both platters in turn under the grill or broiler until the towel begins to steam. If the grill is not big enough for this treatment, reheat the platters, uncovered, for 5 or so minutes in a 190°C/375°F/gas mark 5 oven, but the beef will cook further.

Serve with coarse salt, mustard, and *cornichons*. The bouillon can be used the following day as a basis for soup, and leftover beef is delicious in mustardy, horseradishy sandwiches.

Soufflé glacé aux canneberges

The texture should be soft and rich with no trace of icy particles. Test with a skewer before serving to check this.

Soufflé

105 g/3½ oz fresh cranberries
A small stick of cinnamon
60 ml/4 tbs ruby port
30 ml/2 tbs water
25 ml/2 conservative tbs crème de cassis (black currant liqueur)

420 ml/14 fl oz/1¾ cups whipping cream
3 eggs
135 g/4½ oz/⅔ cup castor (granulated) sugar flavoured by a week's contact with a split vanilla bean

Topping

300 ml/½ pint/1¼ cups alcoholic sweet cider, sparkling or still
A small stick of cinnamon
A small pinch of grated nutmeg
180 ml/6 fl oz/¾ cup fruity red wine

The juice of half a lemon
The grated zest of an orange
Granulated sugar to taste
180 g/6 oz fresh cranberries

Macaroons or langues de chat biscuits

To make the soufflé, place the cranberries and cinnamon stick in a saucepan and add the port and water. Poach the cranberries until they pop; remove cinnamon, drain berries, chop roughly, and dry thoroughly. Meanwhile reduce the poaching liquid to 25 ml/2 modest tbs, then add the *crème de cassis* off the heat and reserve.

Beat the cream until stiff but not grainy, and chill it. Separate the eggs and beat the yolks with half the vanilla sugar to a frothy, white mass. Beat the whites to peaks, gradually beat in the remaining sugar and whisk until very stiff and shiny. Fold together the three elements, adding the *crème de cassis* syrup. When the mixture is well combined but retains its volume, lightly stir in the chopped cranberries. Pile into a soufflé dish of 13 cm/5 in diameter wrapped with a high paper collar secured by paperclips. Freeze uncovered, overnight.

Prepare the topping by putting all its ingredients except the cranberries into a saucepan. Stir well, add the berries, and poach very gently – tasting for sugar – until they burst. Take immediately from the heat, leave the mixture for 3 hours, then remove the stick of cinnamon.

Place the soufflé in the refrigerator to soften about 2 hours before serving. Just before bringing it to the table, top with some of the poached cranberries and remove the collar. Serve the remaining cranberries in a bowl accompanied by macaroons or *langues de chat*.

Lyn Hall, Richmond, Surrey, England

A meal with Italian overtones
for six to eight

ANTIPASTI

ROAST LOIN OF VEAL
STUFFED WITH MUSHROOMS AND FOIE GRAS

PURÉES OF CAULIFLOWER AND CURRY,
CARROT AND RICE

CANNOLI

A meal with Italian overtones
for six to eight

Another dinner that's not exactly modest, and if not entirely Italian, emphatically so in first and last courses.

Marcella Hazan calls *antipasti* "the rogues of the Italian table", their showy variety seducing many a patron of *trattorie* who had planned to have just a *little* something. *Antipasti* in variety are indeed a tradition of Italian restaurants rather than homes, where the midday meal may start with one or two simple dishes of olives, sausage or ham, fish, or prepared vegetables. So here's a chance to pull out the stops and make a display of four rather ambitious *antipasti* served all at once or – of greater interest – in succession to heighten contrasting colours and textures. Each should yield a few mouthfuls per person.

The well *foie-gras*'d veal from Virginia Jones of Tokyo must be young, pale, and milk-fed, not the reddish baby beef which sometimes passes as veal. Our two vegetable purées have a certain simplicity and are not averse to mopping up a little of the neighbouring sauce.

Then *cannoli*, a famous Sicilian dessert of fried pastry and ricotta cheese that parades through numerous windows of Palermo *pasticcerie*. Again, rarely part of home cooking, except in America where I've once or twice been served them at the end of dinner.

The *antipasti* can be offered hot, warm, or at room temperature – with the exception of *carpaccio* which of course is cold. So time them to suit your wishes. The veal can be given its preliminary browning a long time ahead, but should be roasted in the two hours before eating, while the vegetable purées are prepared early and reheated with a little cream. Make the *cannoli* shells and filling in the morning and put them together

102

when the veal plates are cleared; assembly takes just a few minutes.

AWS

The resources of David and Virginia Jones' cellar are considerable, as I discovered on my first visit to Japan. When they invited some fellow members of our Tokyo branch to judge the veal, David stylishly served *two* classified bordeaux – a Léoville-Las-Cases of St-Julien and a Giscours from Labarde. Not bad! However, we have the task of proposing wine both for Gail Wright's piquant "rogues" and that operatic veal *farce* of *foie gras*, kidneys and mushrooms, so our thoughts grow more and more Italian.

The Romans of course believed that their empire spanned the world and would last forever. So a reincarnation of Marcus Apicius, the celebrated gourmand of the time of Augustus and Tiberius, would probably show little surprise that 1900 years later we should gather recipes from Londinium as well as unknown colonies like New York, Tokyo and Columbus, Ohio.

No doubt he would learn with pleasure of grapes called nebbiolo and sangiovese flourishing in Australia, of "chianti" fermenting in Mexico, and of wine-makers in California with names like Parducci and Foppiano!

Which logically brings my mind to the Napa Valley: for the *antipasti*, Monticello chardonnay; with the veal, the immense Heitz grignolino, its grape a triumph of Italo-American co-operation. And then, Mondavi's Moscato d'Oro, a superb fresh dessert wine, perfumed like apricots, with which to caress the *cannoli*!

Readers confined to European, African or antipodean suppliers will not find it hard to discover alternatives.

HD-M

Antipasti

Zucchine ripiene – Stuffed courgettes

4 medium-sized courgettes (*zucchini*)	*Two 15-ml spoons/2 tbs each chopped cooked ham, fresh breadcrumbs, and thick cream*
About 90 g/3 oz freshly-grated cheese – perhaps a combination of Parmesan and another milder one	Salt and pepper Dried breadcrumbs Olive oil

Wash the courgettes and halve them across, then halve them lengthwise to make each courgette into four pieces. Carefully scoop out the central cores to create sixteen boat shapes and dry these with kitchen paper. Mix the cheese, ham, fresh breadcrumbs, and cream, season well, and pack the stuffing firmly into the boats. Place these in a lightly-oiled baking dish, strew the tops with dried breadcrumbs and dribble on a little olive oil. Bake the courgettes for 30–40 minutes at 190°C/375°F/gas mark 5 until the tops are golden-brown. Serve hot, or at room temperature, in bite-size pieces.

These may be assembled in advance, covered with plastic wrap, then baked at the last minute. The addition of a little chopped garlic to the stuffing would not come amiss.

Carpaccio – Marinated raw beef
A similar recipe was sent to us by John Bruno of the black bean soup on page 87.

A 420 g/14 oz piece of rump steak	*Salt and pepper*
or boneless loin or rib steak	*Fontina or similar full-bodied*
Olive oil	*pressed cheese*
1 small onion	*White truffle, if possible*
Juice of 1½ lemons	

Trim the beef of all fat and connective tissue and slice it as thinly as possible, across the grain – chill the meat in the freezer for an hour, if necessary, to facilitate this. Place each slice between two sheets of cellophane or plastic wrap and use a rolling pin to roll the meat as thin as Parma ham, or pound it out carefully with a mallet.

Pour enough oil to cover the bottom of a large, flat plate and lay the slices on top. Peel and finely mince the onion and sprinkle it, with strained lemon juice, over the meat. Add salt and pepper and sufficient oil to coat lightly.

Allow the beef to marinate for about 2 hours at room temperature, then garnish it with slivers of cheese and the de luxe white truffle if the latter is available – and affordable!

Frittata – Open-faced Italian omelette
480 g/1 lb spinach, stemmed	*Salt and pepper*
3 eggs	*Butter*

Cook and drain the spinach, press out all moisture, and chop it. Whisk the eggs, add the spinach and season well. Melt a little butter in an omelette or heavy frying pan, add the egg mixture and cook it very slowly until the eggs have set and only the top is runny. Hold the pan under the grill or broiler until the top sets and is just beginning to colour.

Serve hot or cool, cut into tiny wedges. Variations using fried onion or lightly-cooked and sliced courgettes and artichoke hearts are recommended.

Peperoni e acciughe – Peppers in an anchovy sauce

3 sweet peppers, ideally one each   10–12 anchovy fillets
   red, yellow, and green   Pepper
About 45 ml/3 tbs olive oil

Open the peppers, trim them, remove the seeds and slice the flesh lengthwise into thin strips. Heat the oil in a heavy sauté pan and fry the strips until they are soft and brown at the edges. With a slotted spoon remove them from the pan, stir the anchovies – thinly sliced lengthwise – into the oil, adding more oil if necessary to make a pouring sauce, and top the peppers with this mixture. Grind on black pepper and serve either hot, warm, or at room temperature.

All recipes from Gail Wright, South Bank branch, London, England

Roast loin of veal stuffed with mushrooms and foie gras

This sumptuous cut should be roasted in a covered casserole to concentrate the juices and flavour of a meat which has little natural fat.

1600 g/3½ lb (boned weight) loin   1 each large carrot and onion
   of milk-fed veal, plus its bones   1 stalk celery
   and some extra ones with meat   60–120 ml/2–4 fl oz/¼–½ cup port
   on them   240–360 ml/8–12 fl oz/1–1½ cups
1 very fresh veal kidney   veal stock made with above
150 g/5 oz mushrooms   bones and appropriate vegetables
75 g/2½ oz butter   and herbs, using the method
Salt and pepper   described on page 220
Oil   Arrowroot (optional)
Cognac or other brandy   Watercress as garnish
105 g/3½ oz foie gras

Have the butcher bone the veal loin and give you the bones – plus extra ones – from which to make the stock that you'll use here.

Remove the fat and membrane from the kidney, cut it in half and then into quarters – or eighths if large – removing the fatty white core. Halve or quarter the mushrooms, depending on size, and wash them well. Melt 15g/½ oz butter in a sauté pan and toss the mushrooms, salted, for a few minutes over a high heat until just cooked. Season them further and drain.

Add a little oil to the mushroom pan, make it hot, season the kidney pieces and cook them *very* quickly – about a minute per side – on the high heat. Add a good dash of brandy, flame it, and remove the kidneys to drain.

Open out the veal, boned side up, incise its heavy end to make this wider, salt and pepper it well.

Put a row of mushrooms – about 5 cm/2 in across – down the centre of the meat.

Cut the *foie gras* into 1½ cm/½ in strips and lay these along the meat beside the mushrooms; place the pieces of kidney atop the fungi.

Form the meat into a roll and tie it with soft white butchers' string at 2½ cm/1 in intervals; tie the ends. Dry the roll and season with salt.

Take a heavy oval cocotte or casserole just big enough for the veal and equipped with a well-fitting lid, melt therein 30 g/1 oz butter with a little oil and brown the meat lightly on all sides. Remove it, clean the pan, melt another 30 g/1 oz butter, and add the peeled, sliced carrot and onion and the cleaned, sliced stalk of celery. Salt, and cook them, covered, over a low heat for five minutes to soften.

Return the veal to the casserole, baste it well with the butter there and cover meat and vegetables closely with a double layer of foil, tucking it well down around them. Put the lid on the casserole and roast in the lower part of a 155°C/310°F/gas mark 2 oven for 1½–1¾ hours, basting the contents three times. The roast is done when it is firm to the touch and a meat thermometer plunged into the centre reads 74°C/165°F.

Let the veal rest on a hot platter while you make the sauce. Degrease the pan juices, put the casserole over a brisk heat, stir and mash the vegetables into the juices, add half the total amounts of port and stock, and boil down the result, adding more of either liquid to achieve the flavour and quantity of sauce that you like.

Cut string from the meat and carve it, overlapping slices and stuffing onto a hot platter.

Season the sauce, strain it into a hot boat (or you can thicken it with a little slaked arrowroot if you prefer, after straining), reheat the meat if necessary – covered with a wet and wrung-out tea towel – under the grill or broiler until the towel begins to steam, pour on a bit of the sauce and serve the veal garnished with watercress and accompanied by the remainder.

Virginia Jones, Tokyo, Japan

Cauliflower and curry purée

A nutty flavour and an interesting texture.

2 large cauliflowers, weighing   60 g/2 oz butter
   about 600 g/1¼ lb each   Mild curry powder
   untrimmed   Pepper
Salt   Thick cream

Bring a large pot of salted water to the boil while trimming cauliflowers of stalks and greenery and cutting the heads into small florets. Boil these

until tender but not mushy - 3–5 minutes - and drain. Let the cauliflower cool slightly, then purée it completely in a food processor.

If the purée seems at all watery, stir it in a saucepan over low heat to dry away the excess moisture.

Shortly before serving, melt the butter in a similar saucepan, add the purée, salt and pepper to taste, and just enough curry powder to *suggest* its flavour without overstatement. Stir in 45–75 ml/3–5 tbs cream, enough to ease and smooth the purée but not to make it runny, heat it through, and serve very hot.

Carrot and rice purée

The rice gives body and a slight grain to a vegetable which might otherwise remind you of baby food.

*720 g/1½ lb carrots, trimmed and
    peeled weight
1 medium clove garlic
840 ml/28 fl oz/3½ cups chicken
    stock or milk
Big pinch thyme*

*Salt
60 g/2 oz rice, short-grain if
    possible
Pepper
15 g/½ oz butter
Thick cream*

Prepare and cut up the carrots, peel and slightly crush garlic and put both into a large heavy saucepan with stock or milk, thyme, and salt. Bring to the boil – slowly if using milk, as the carrots' acidity can cause it to curdle – stir in the rice and simmer, covered, for about 20 minutes or until the carrots and rice are tender. Let the mixture cool slightly, drain, reserving the liquid, and purée the carrots and rice in the food processor, adding a little liquid to loosen consistency. Season.

Shortly before serving, reheat the purée with butter in a heavy saucepan, stir in 30–45 ml/2–3 tbs thick cream and more of the stock or milk if necessary, adjust seasoning, and serve very hot.

Cannoli

This recipe makes about 18–20 pieces, and you will need to use *cannoli* tubes – metal cylinders of 15 cm/6 in length by 2 cm/¾ in across.

Shells

210 g/7 oz/scant 1½ cups plain
flour
A pinch of salt
One 15-ml spoon/1 tbs castor
(granulated) sugar

30 g/1 oz firm butter
A scant 90 ml/bare 3 fl oz/
generous ⅓ cup marsala wine
Part of a beaten egg
Oil for deep frying

Filling

360 g/12 oz very fresh
ricotta (whey) cheese, or half
ricotta and half curd, or all curd
cheese if fresh ricotta is
unavailable
105 g/3½ oz/scant ¾ cup icing
(confectioners') sugar

About 2.5-ml/½ tsp vanilla extract
Almond extract to taste
45 g/1½ oz each shelled pistachios
and coarsely-grated semi-sweet
chocolate
Extra chopped pistachios

To make the shells, sift together flour, salt, and sugar, cut or rub in the butter to form fine particles. Add the marsala and enough of the beaten egg to make a soft dough that's not sticky. Knead the dough on a floured board for about 5 minutes, or until smooth and elastic. Cover and let stand for at least an hour.

On a large floured surface, roll the dough into a paper-thin sheet. Cut this into 13 cm/5 in circles and wrap each round a lightly-floured *cannoli* tube, pressing the dough to seal overlapping edges.

Pre-heat the frying oil to 195°C/380°F and deep-fry several *cannoli* at a time until crisp and golden-brown. Drain them on kitchen paper and when *cannoli* are tepid, carefully turn and slide out the tubes and proceed to make the next batch.

Prepare the filling by beating the cheese and sugar until smooth, add the two extracts, the skinned and chopped pistachios and the chocolate. Lightly chill the mixture, and just before serving, use a wide-tipped pastry bag to pipe it into each shell. Sprinkle the visible filling with extra chopped pistachios.

As a change, you might replace the combined pistachios and chocolate with some minced candied fruits.

Elvira M. Serra, Columbus, Ohio Wine & Food Society, USA

Game for two

ŒUFS DE CAILLE AU CRESSON
Soft-boiled quails' eggs, watercress purée

RÂBLE DE LIÈVRE À LA DIANE
Roast saddle of hare

CRÈME DE MARRONS EN BARQUETTES
Skiffs of chestnut purée
POIRES AU VIN ROUGE
Pears poached in red wine

TARTES AUX POMMES EN LAMELLES
A pair of hot apple tarts

LE PAIN BÉNIT D'ÉCOSSE
Haggis on toast

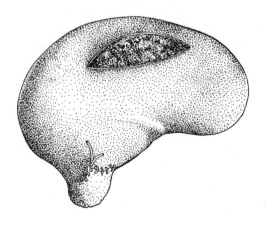

Game for two

Of all the meals in this book, here is the one I would most like to have someone cook for me – ideally Guy Mouilleron, owner of Ma Cuisine, the tiny one-starred London restaurant where I was once a chef and whose food is delectable. His roast saddle of hare, named for the goddess of hunting and served with a subtle, mustardy sauce plus chestnut purée and vinous pears, is the *clou*, the star attraction of this very French evening that ends with a tribute to the Franco-Scots connection.

Give this dinner as a present to your game-loving spouse or *grand amour*, have it made in your kitchen by Guy or his equivalent, or by a friend who happens to cook superbly and will serve discreetly. Or, if you do it yourself, dress simply and work with a light heart because almost everything must be prepared *à la minute* – "to order", as they say backstage.

Quails' eggs on a bed of blanched watercress and chives turned in vinaigrette are like an appetiser for the hare served very rare, its fillets carved across the grain and reassembled on the bone. The beast should be a young one – *de l'année* – at its best after the first hard frosts, and of course, itself never frozen. Hare requires escorts that are not too creamy; chestnuts contribute the right farinaceous quality, and pears poached in wine, lemon, and cinnamon add some sweet-sharp notes.

To follow, the thinnest individual apple tarts of puff pastry, assembled and baked to be ready when you are, and then – *tradition brittanique* returns – the savoury *pain bénit d'Écosse* to the French, and haggis on toast to Maurice Kidd, who put it on the menu of a 1952 Edinburgh Wine & Food Society dinner at the request of André Simon.

112

For many of you, recital of the recipe will substitute for eating it, which – take it from two connoisseurs of haggis – is a very great pity.

The only aspects of this meal which can be finished early are the pastry *barquettes*, the chestnut purée (without its cream), the pears, the game stock for the hare's sauce, the *feuilleté* rounds (uncooked) – and of course the haggis, which is reheated in simmering water to serve.

AWS

I hope your aperitif for this banquet will be champagne. Since you might keep a little back for the quails' eggs, a full bottle seems justified; and if you should forget that intention, no matter – they will slide down quite easily without. The hare is an occasion for a bottle of your best red burgundy or côte rôtie or an old *gran reserva* rioja. In Australia, an aged bottle of Lake's Folly from the Hunter Valley would be bonzer, or in America, one of Joe Heitz's incomparable cabernet sauvignons.

The apple tart calls for its own wine, but not too much, since you may have further plans for the evening – and so have we, for the haggis is yet to come! A small glass each of sauternes perhaps, or if you prefer something sweeter, an Italian moscato or a rich Hungarian tokay.

For Maurice Kidd, a founder member of the Society, there is only one beverage to match the haggis: a glass of fine old malt whisky, "the

Presbyterian wine". He recommends Cardhu, while conceding that there are several worthy substitutes. We reckon he would not consider Dutch or Australian "whiskies" among them, but in our opinion (since we aren't Scots) *Irish* whiskey would make a perfectly acceptable alternative.

HD-M

Œufs de caille au cresson

The cress and chives should be available during winter in areas supplied by hot-house growers.

A 240 g/8 oz bunch of very fresh watercress
A few pungent leaves, if obtainable, like cultivated dandelion or escarole

30 g/1 oz fresh chives
5 ml/1 teasp lemon juice
Salt and pepper
15-ml/1 tbs mild olive oil
8 fresh quails' eggs

Remove stems from the cress by means of a smart twist, discard the stems and reserve six perfect leaves for garnish. Cut up the pungent leaves and scissor chives into short lengths. Wash all three and plunge everything to simmer for 30 seconds in boiling salted water. Drain, refresh, and whiz the greenery in a salad dryer, or squeeze it to remove the excess water. Make a not-too-fine purée in the food processor and squeeze the residual water from this.

Make a vinaigrette with the lemon juice, salt, pepper, and oil. Turn the greens in *just* enough of this to give them flavour without any excess (use the surplus vinaigrette for something else), and make a bed of the greens in the centre of two small plates.

Bring a saucepan of water to the boil and lower into it the 8 eggs. Give them 2 minutes' full simmer, remove them with a slotted spoon (replace the saucepan over a low heat), refresh in cold water, crack the shells, peel very carefully (6 eggs are needed for this dish – the extra 2 are in case of mishaps), working fast; the eggs will have a set white and a soft yolk and are therefore fragile. Rinse them, plunge them back into the pan of water – which should be just below the simmer – and reheat for about 15 seconds.

Drain the eggs well and arrange a cluster of three each on the beds of cress, grind on salt and pepper, garnish each plate with three leaves of watercress, and serve fast.

Râble de lièvre à la Diane

Ideally a little aged, or *rassis*, the hare, says Guy Mouilleron, should be hung by the feet, ungutted, in its skin – from which it takes flavour – for two days after death, then skinned and gutted and held for two days further in the bottom of your refrigerator. Of course, you may avoid such goings-on by ordering the appropriate hare from your butcher or by taking him the one you've shot and asking that he deal with it.

A young hare, as described
Olive oil
Black peppercorns
2 leaves of sage
Wine vinegar infused with raspberries or black currants
1 each carrot, medium onion, and large clove garlic

Parsley stalks
Mushroom peelings (optional)
A large glass of robust red wine
Salt
Thick cream
French mustard, preferably Dijon
Pepper

Remove the *râble* – the saddle – on its spine, from the hare – or ask the butcher to do this and to give you the rest of the hare, its blood in some vinegar to prevent curdling, and all of its trimmings.

With the aid of a flexible knife, remove the nervous membrane from the upper saddle meat without detaching flesh from the bone. Rub the saddle all over with some olive oil to nourish it, put it into a shallow glass or china container with a bit more oil, a few peppercorns, the sage leaves, and a little wine vinegar. Leave the saddle overnight, basting occasionally.

Use the hare's fore and hind legs and blood in the Scots hare soup on page 202, in a *civet de lièvre* or a jugged hare, or (minus its blood) in a game pâté. Take the head, off-cuts, and any spare bones to make a good hare stock or *fond de gibier* for the *râble* sauce, as follows.

Cut this miscellany into manageable pieces and put them into a heavy roasting pan with the peeled carrot, the unpeeled onion and garlic, all cut up small, plus the parsley stalks, and the mushroom peelings if you have them. Roast these "dry" in a 205°C/400°F/gas mark 6 oven, stirring them several times until they've begun to brown. Deglaze the pan with the red wine and 30 ml/2 tbs vinegar, transfer all to a heavy saucepan, cover well with water, add a little salt, and simmer gently for one hour. Strain the stock, pressing against the vegetables, and reduce it to give a *fond de gibier* of about 300 ml/½ pint/1¼ cups.

When you are ready, take the saddle from its oil, wipe it dry, season, and put it into a small heavy roasting or sauté pan with an ovenproof handle and then into a 245°C/475°F/gas mark 9 oven to roast for 12–15 minutes, depending on its size. The result should be very rare.

Remove the saddle and put it into a covered dish in a warm place to rest for 10 minutes. Deglaze the pan with 5 ml/1 teasp vinegar, add the *fond de gibier* and let reduce a little, transferring it to a small saucepan if more convenient. Add 30–45 ml/2–3 tbs thick cream, gently reduce for 5 minutes more, add mustard, perhaps as much as a 5-ml spoon/1 teasp, and simmer for a few moments. Judge consistency of the sauce – it should just coat a spoon's back – and decide whether to add a drop more mustard; adjust the seasoning, add the blood which has fallen from the resting saddle, and don't boil the sauce again. Strain and keep it hot in a *bain-marie* while carving the hare.

Take a sharp carving knife and cut down one side of the hare's backbone, following its contour, to remove intact one loin fillet. Do the same with the other side, turn the bone over and remove the two small fillets from underneath. Put the backbone right side up on a hot platter, carve the smaller, then the larger fillets a fat $\frac{3}{4}$ cm/$\frac{1}{4}$ in thick, on the bias, reassemble the larger fillets along either side of the backbone with the carved *filets mignons* beneath the bone to steady it, and if necessary, reheat the platter under a wet and wrung tea-towel beneath the grill or broiler, as for the roast loin of veal in the preceding recipe. Game cools very quickly. Pour a little sauce over the saddle and serve the rest in a sauceboat on a second heated platter surrounded by *barquettes* of *marron* and the pears poached in red wine.

Crème de marrons en barquettes

There is no need here to shell fresh chestnuts – a long and tedious task – when you can buy whole unsweetened ones in tins. Avoid the ready-made canned purée, which lacks character.

120 g/4 oz shortcrust I (page 222)	*Butter*
A can of whole unsweetened	*Cream*
chestnuts in water, weighing	*Salt and pepper*
about 440 g/a scant 15 oz,	
undrained	

Roll out the pastry and line 6–8 metal tartlet moulds in the shape of *barquettes* or small rowboats (round ones will substitute but are not so pretty), chill, and bake them as for carrot and poppy tartlets on page 156, baking the pastry until fully cooked. These should be done in the morning for the evening.

Drain the chestnuts of their water and purée them completely in the food processor. While the saddle is resting after roasting, heat the purée, with just enough butter and cream to make it smooth and fluffy, season it, and serve very hot in the pastry skiffs.

Poires au vin rouge

2 hard pears	*Granulated sugar*
½ a lemon	*A cinnamon stick*
Robust red wine	

Peel, halve, and core the pears, rub them all over with the lemon's cut surface to prevent discoloration, put them into a small saucepan and cover with red wine. Add about 60 g/4½ tbs of sugar, a long strip of lemon zest without the pith, and the cinnamon stick. Bring the wine to the boil, swirling to dissolve sugar, lower the heat, cover the pan and poach the pears for a few minutes until they are *just* tender. If making in advance, cool all in a covered bowl, refrigerate, and then reheat fruit gently in the wine. Drain very well, and serve the pears with the chestnut *barquettes* and the boat of sauce.

All three recipes from Guy Mouilleron, London, England

Tartes aux pommes en lamelles

A *lamelle* is a leaf-thin sheet or layer, like these slim leaves of apple on rounds of puff pastry.

180 g/6 oz puff pastry (page 223)	*Castor or granulated sugar*
2 firm eating apples	*Thick cream whipped with a little*
Butter, unsalted if possible	*sugar and a dash of brandy*

Cut off the weight of puff that you'll need, give it two more turns, rest it if necessary, then roll the pastry to a thickness of about $\frac{1}{4}$ cm/$\frac{1}{16}$ in. With a 16 cm/6$\frac{1}{2}$ in plate as a guide, cut out two rounds. Flip the rounds over onto a slightly moist baking sheet, prick them with a fork, and refrigerate for thirty minutes. This can be done some hours in advance if you cover the rounds once they have firmed. Use the pastry off-cuts for another purpose.

When ready, core, peel, and slice the apples very, very thinly. Overlap slices in rows down each round so that all the pastry is covered, dot the apple sparingly with bits of butter, sprinkle with sugar, and bake the *tartes* in a 205°C/400°F/gas mark 6 oven for 25 or so minutes until cooked and golden. Run them briefly under the grill or broiler to caramelise the apples' edges if need be, and serve pronto, with a bowl of lightly sugared and brandied whipped cream.

Le pain bénit d'Écosse

In Maurice Kidd's own words:

> Prepare and cook a haggis in the usual way [heart, liver, and "lights" or lungs of lamb or mutton, oatmeal, suet, onions, seasoning, and stock, poached for several hours in a sheep's paunch or a muslin bag – AWS] with a preference for deer's liver instead of lamb's. Toast and butter small pieces of brown bread on which place large spoonfuls of hot haggis. Serve this savoury with a glass of Highland malt whisky.

Maurice Kidd, East Lothian, Scotland

A meal with Oriental flavouring
for four

SARDINE AND SEAWEED PUFFS, BEURRE FONDU

MIXED VEGETABLES IN GADO-GADO SAUCE

CHICKEN STIR-FRIED WITH VEGETABLES
AND OYSTER SAUCE

SQUID CHINESE-STYLE
FRIED NOODLES

BOILED OR STEAMED RICE

CHERRY BOUNCE WITH VANILLA ICE CREAM IN TRICORN
HATS

A meal with Oriental flavouring
for four

When it comes to Oriental food, Hugo and I are enthusiastic laymen, loving its mystery and finesse but knowing little, from first-hand experience, about its cooking. So thanks to Hiang Lim Holtom of London, originally from Sarawak in Malaysia, and Jack Witter of New South Wales, we have a menu with an Oriental centre based on vegetables, chicken, and squid.

As it happens, Haruhiko Kamogawa, Japan's leading wine writer, had brought Hugo and me a box of *nori*, the Japanese dried seaweed; here indeed was some Oriental flavouring. So we dreamed up a variation on a recipe of Peter Kromberg's, the very inventive chef of Le Soufflé Restaurant at London's Inter-Continental Hotel, using sardines and fresh coriander where Peter puts salmon and sea-scallops, and saucing the seaweed-flecked cushions of puff pastry with some julienned vegetables and a *beurre fondu* – literally "melted butter" – the frothing emulsion of butter and water. These puffs, as you construct them, suggest Japanese patterns, and the seaweed adds dimensions of mystery and smoke to the fish.

Hiang proposed that the next three dishes, plus plenty of boiled or steamed rice, be placed on the table all at once – or as near simultaneously as you can manage – the stir-fried chicken, squid and their noodles, plus rice, being kept hot on heaters as they arrive. The cook, having tossed and stir-fried at a gallop, can then sit down and tuck in without distraction. The mixed vegetables in their rather fiery peanut-based *gado-gado* sauce are eaten cold. Ingredients like seaweed, dried tamarinds, shrimp paste, bean curd, oyster sauce and so on are available from Chinese supermarkets, and if you don't have a *wok*, use instead a wide – and if possible, deep – frying pan.

120

Cherry bounce – sugared cherries in spirits – plus vanilla ice cream, served in a brittle biscuit (biscuit in the British sense) shaped like a tricorn hat, is obviously not part of the Oriental pattern! It's an easy and stimulating way to end a labour-intensive meal.

The puffs and their julienned trimming can be made in the morning and cooked as you whisk the *beurre fondu* to start the meal. The vegetables can stand for several hours in their *gado-gado* sauce to blend flavours – or the sauce can be added as you serve – but chicken and squid, whose ingredients will of course have been lined up early, must be cooked *à la minute*. The dessert is a work of fast assembly.

AWS

One of the most interesting things about the advent of the so-called *nouvelle cuisine* has been the need it imposed on chefs to re-examine their attitudes to Oriental cookery. In the search for ways of bringing out the essential qualities of good ingredients, no one could ignore the delicacy of flavour and presentation achieved by Eastern cooks. Gastronomically, East meets West more and more these days.

One result of this has been an abandonment of the old belief that *no* wine could match the intricacies of Oriental food. I assume this misconception arose because of the – quite unnecessary – "jumble" in which some Chinese restaurants serve all their dishes. But if the family of wines is endowed with a whole range of aromas and tastes, so there has to be something that's appropriate, however rarefied the dish and wherever its origin. It's only the knock-out foods like coffee and curry which have no suitable vinous partner. The late Peter Sellers doubtless had this problem in mind when he dreamed up "chocolate-flavoured Wagga Wagga" – a liquid I was sad not to see on any wine list when the Society held its international convention in Australia!

In a memorable article for the American magazine *Gourmet* of February 1975, the California-based wine writer Gerald Asher described an evening of experiments at Helen Kan's San Francisco restaurant in which seven of her most popular dishes, each presenting a different aspect of Chinese cooking, were matched with various wines. The most successful marriages paired prawns in black bean sauce and a chenin blanc from the Napa Valley's Don Chappellet, and spicy Peking beef with Jadot's Beaune Theurons. Much less satisfactory as a companion to sweet-and-sour pork was gewürztraminer (the wine most commonly offered with Chinese dishes, I find), which Gerald described as "an unnecessary baroque flourish totally unrelated to the food". There you have challenge!

Following is a list of the bottles we have tasted and enjoyed with

Eastern cooking: badenwein from Germany, vernaccia from Tuscany, South African steen, wines made from the sauvignon or the grenache grapes, reds from Sicily or the Roussillon in France, and rosés from Corsica and the Italian Tyrol.

So the field is wide open.

HD-M

Sardine and seaweed puffs, beurre fondu

If you can't get whole sardines, substitute anchovies; the fillets of 12–14 of these should do. If neither is available, try pieces of fresh herring fillet or even mackerel; a fairly oily fish of distinctive character is called for. Japanese dried seaweed is sold in packets of dark and iridescent greeny-brown leaves, each leaf measuring round about 10 × 23 cm/4 × 9 in. Substitute Korean or Chinese versions from an Oriental supermarket if the Japanese is not to hand.

6 whole sardines, each about 15–18 cm/6–7 in long, either fresh or frozen (but not canned), and carefully thawed if frozen
90 g/3 oz piece of fat cucumber
A small bunch of fresh coriander leaves or flat-leaf parsley if the former is unavailable
4 thin crêpes of about 15 cm/6 in diameter, either made with a small quantity of the crêpes Suzette batter (minus its sugar)
on page 214, or bought from the Chinese supermarket
480 g/1 lb puff pastry (page 223)
Salt and pepper
A leaf of nori, the Japanese dried seaweed
1 egg yolk
120 g/4 oz each peeled carrots and trimmed white part of leek
120 g/4 oz cold, hard butter, unsalted if possible, and cut into pieces
30 ml/2 tbs dry white wine

Scale and de-fin the sardines, cut off their heads, cut open the bellies, pull out the viscera and rinse the fish inside and out. Cut each fish into its bottom and top fillets, remove the tail, trim the fillets and pull out the small whiskery bones. Leave the skin on, rinse and dry the 12 pieces.

Peel the section of cucumber, cut it in half lengthwise, seed it, and cut each half into thin strips. Dry these in kitchen paper.

Wash the coriander or parsley, dry the leaves, and keep them whole; separate the *crêpes*.

Give the puff pastry its final pair of turns, rest it if necessary, and roll it to a thickness of about ½ cm/⅛ in. Cut it into 4 rectangles of 15 × 20 cm/6 × 8 in each.

Put a *crêpe* onto the centre of each rectangle, place 2 sardine fillets, flesh side up, across each *crêpe*'s lower half, grind on salt and pepper. Divide the strips of cucumber among the 4 puffs, strewing them over the fish, top cucumber with 4 or 5 coriander or parsley leaves per puff, add more seasoning, place the remaining sardine fillet, skin up, over the leaves – as for a sandwich – shred the seaweed and scatter it over the 4 fillings.

Fold in the sides of each *crêpe*, paint the pastry edges with the egg yolk beaten in a little water, and fold each pastry over its filling. Press together the edges, seal them with a fork, trim them neatly, and brush the tops with more yolk.

Rinse a heavy baking sheet with cold water, give it a shake, and carefully transfer the puffs to this. Refrigerate for at least half an hour, or all day if more convenient.

Cut the carrot and leeks into very fine julienne strips.

When ready to go, score the top of each puff with 3 light, diagonal cuts that release a little steam as the pastries cook. Bake in a 205°C/400°F/gas mark 6 oven for about 25 minutes, until the "cushions" are golden-brown and well-risen.

Meanwhile, make a *beurre fondu*. Bring 45 ml/3 tbs of water to the boil in a wide, heavy saucepan. Add 2–3 pieces of the chilled butter, and shaking the pan gently over the heat, let the water boil further. As the butter begins to melt, start whisking. Remove the pan from the heat and gradually whisk in the remaining butter, returning pan to the fire two or three times as you beat. A thick froth will result. Season it, and keep the sauce warm in a *bain-marie* until the puffs are ready.

About 10 minutes before they emerge from the oven, put the julienned carrot and leek into a small heavy saucepan with the white wine, cover, and let the vegetables steam over a low heat until tender but still crisp. Remove the pan's lid to evaporate the wine, and season well.

Serve each puff on a dinner plate, with a generous spoonful of vegetables attractively arranged to one side, next to a spoonful of sauce. Pass the remaining "melted butter" in a warmed boat.

Mixed vegetables in gado-gado sauce

A 100 g/generous 3 oz package of
  dried tamarind fruit
480 g/1 lb roasted peanuts
About 45 ml/3 tbs peanut oil
3 medium onions
1 large clove garlic
One 15-ml spoon/1 tbs chili
  powder
One 5-ml spoon/1 teasp shrimp
  paste

About 360 ml/12 fl oz/1½ cups
  water
75 g/5 tbs castor (granulated)
  sugar
Salt
150 g/5 oz each fresh bean curd,
  raw peeled celery and carrots,
  bean sprouts

Cover the dried tamarinds with 180 ml/6 fl oz/¾ cup water, bring to the boil, and when the water turns a deep caramel colour (after about 20 seconds' simmer), drain and put aside the fruits and reserve the liquid.

Toss the peanuts in 30 ml/1 tbs of the oil in a *wok* – with or without a ring, as you choose – or frying pan over a high heat to colour them further and impart a slightly "burnt" flavour. Cool and grind them coarsely.

Peel and chop onions and garlic, and with the help of a little oil, blend them to a paste in a blender or food processor. Heat the remaining peanut oil in the *wok* or frying pan and fry this paste over a moderate heat with the chili powder and shrimp paste. Add the ground peanuts, the water, and the tamarind water. Simmer this for 10–15 minutes, adding more water if necessary to get a loose-textured sauce; add sugar and salt and cool.

Sliver the bean curd, cut the celery and carrots into large matchsticks, and put them with the bean sprouts onto a platter. Pour over the cooled *gado-gado* sauce.

Hiang Holtom, South Bank branch, London, England

Chicken stir-fried with vegetables and oyster sauce

1 small onion
1 large clove garlic
2 slices fresh, peeled ginger root
120 g/4 oz each chicken meat,
   cauliflower florets, mushrooms,
   and fresh chicken livers
Half a sweet red pepper
45 g/1½ oz cashew nuts

30 ml/2 tbs peanut oil
One 5-ml spoon/1 teasp cornflour
   (cornstarch)
15 ml/1 tbs oyster sauce
120 g/4 oz bean sprouts
Salt and pepper
15 ml/1 tbs sake wine or dry
   sherry

Have all the ingredients prepared in advance: peel and finely chop the
onion and garlic, sliver the ginger, cut the chicken into bite-size pieces,
thinly slice the cauliflower florets, mushrooms, chicken livers, and the
cleaned and seeded pepper half. Roast the cashews for several minutes
in a 180°C/350°F/gas mark 4 oven to bring up their colour.

Then fry the onion, garlic, and ginger in a pre-heated oiled wok –
with or without its ring – or frying-pan until they are browning, stirring
with chopsticks or a small wooden spatula and tossing the whole time.
Add the chicken meat and stir-fry for 2 minutes. Add all the vegetables
except the bean sprouts, stir and toss for a further 3 minutes.

Slake the cornflour (cornstarch) in the oyster sauce, add to the *wok* with the sliced livers and cook for 2 minutes, add the bean sprouts and stir-fry a minute longer. Season to taste, mix in nuts and wine and serve immediately.

Hiang Holtom

Squid Chinese-style

Don't be alarmed at the notion of ginger root twice at one sitting; the effect here is quite different.

One or more squid, fresh or
  frozen, totalling about 500 g/
  17 oz in weight
900 ml/1½ pints/1 quart fish broth
  made from squid trimmings
A small piece of fresh ginger root
5 spring onions (scallions)
90 g/3 oz green French beans
Two 5-ml spoons/2 teasp cornflour
  (cornstarch)

60 g/2 oz pine nuts or blanched
  slivered almonds
30 ml/2 tbs whisky
15 ml/1 tbs dark soy sauce
Salt and pepper
Fresh Chinese noodles, more
  chopped spring onions
  (scallions), fish sauce

Prepare all the ingredients in advance. Wash the squid (well-thawed, if frozen), draw the quill from its body pouch, pull the head and body apart. The viscera and ink sac will come away with the head. Skin the body pouch and fins, open up the body and pull away the mucous membrane. Cut the tentacles away from the squid's head, discard head, ink sac, viscera, and quill. Cut up the tentacles and use them to make the fish broth. Slice the squid pouch and fins into short, slim strips. Repeat with other squid if using more than one.

Peel the ginger root and grate about one 5-ml spoon/1 teasp of it. Clean and trim the spring onions or scallions, cut their white and some of the green into slim rings.

String the beans if necessary, thinly slice them on the diagonal. Slake the cornflour or cornstarch in a little of the fish broth.

When ready, poach the squid strips gently in the broth for about 10 minutes or until they turn completely opaque. Remove from the broth with a slotted spoon.

Heat a *wok* on its ring – or a deep frying-pan – very hot, pour in 240 ml/8 fl oz/1 cup fish broth, add the ginger, and boil for a few seconds.

Stirring continuously, add the squid, onions, beans, nuts, whisky, soy sauce, and dissolved cornflour, plus as much additional fish broth as you judge necessary, and boil until the cornflour thickens and has cooked. Season, grate in more ginger if you like, and serve immediately. Hiang Holtom suggests you accompany this with *wok*-fried Chinese noodles garnished by chopped spring onions or scallions and a drop of fish sauce.

J. A. Witter, New South Wales Wine & Food Society, Australia

Cherry bounce with vanilla ice cream in tricorn hats

The bounce can be made with raspberries instead of cherries, and should mature for a minimum of three months before use. Barbara Holland says that two years' soaking is ideal!

2 kg/4¼ lbs fresh sour cherries in perfect condition
Castor or "superfine" or finely granulated sugar

Roughly 1½ litres/2½ pints/1½ quarts first-class brandy or vodka; have more handy, as you may need it

Wash, stem, and pit the cherries. Dry them thoroughly on kitchen paper.
    Sterilise clamp-top glass jars or those with two-piece metal lids – lids and fittings included. Let them dry, and while they're still hot, start stocking them with alternating layers of cherries and sugar until the jars are filled to 1½ cm/½ in from the top. Carefully pour on the spirits and wipe away any that would come into contact with the lids. Clamp or screw these on. Allow the jars to cool, store them in a dry, dark place and forget them for the requisite months or years.
    When ready to use, spoon some of the fruit and juice over vanilla ice cream that has been scooped into tricorn "hats".

Barbara D. Holland, Columbus, Ohio Wine & Food Society, USA

Tricorns
This batter makes eight pieces. You can consider the first few as

practice, or if successful from the beginning, you'll have enough for second helpings.

60 g/2 oz butter, preferably
  unsalted
120 g/4 oz/a scant ⅔ cup castor
  (granulated) sugar

60 g/7 tbs plain flour
Pinch of salt, if butter is unsalted
3 egg whites
A dash of vanilla extract

Melt the butter and beat in the sugar, crumble in the sifted flour and salt (if included). Beat the egg whites to break them up, and combine these, plus vanilla, with the buttery base. Sieve this mixture.

Cut baking parchment to fit a heavy baking sheet and draw on it two 18 cm/7 in circles. Invert and lightly oil the paper.

Drop a good 15-ml spoon/1 tbs of batter onto each circle and spread both spoonfuls very thin with the back of a wet dessertspoon. Bake at 190°C/375°F/gas mark 5 for 8 minutes, or until biscuits are golden and browning.

Have ready a glass jar of about 6½ cm/2½ in diameter, inverted and oiled on the base and exterior. With a flexible spatula or palette knife, gently loosen one biscuit from the paper – biscuit may stick but it won't break – and return it to the oven on the papered sheet for 30 seconds to re-soften. Then quickly shape it – right side down – on the jar, gently pressing the centre and moulding the sides into a sort of tricorn hat. Keep the second biscuit warm inside the oven with the door ajar, and when the first one has hardened, remove it from the jar and form the next one in the same way.

Continue like this with the remaining batter, renewing paper if necessary, and when all the tricorns are ready and cooled, store them carefully in a large airtight tin.

Eat within a few days of making. If you find that they've softened and lost their ripple while in the tin, simply reheat them briefly, one at a time, in a medium oven and reshape them on the oiled jar.

Occasions

A late Sunday breakfast
for four

RUM OMELETTE SOUFFLÉ

WATERGRUWEL
Barley with currants and raisins

SALLY LUNN

MARROW LEMON PRESERVE
QUINCE JELLY

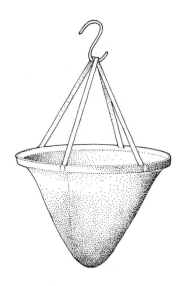

A late Sunday breakfast
for four

Julius Wile of New York, having accomplished the careers of wine shipper, merchant, and writer – he has, for instance, edited the recent editions of Frank Schoonmaker's *Encyclopedia of Wine* – has now, in retirement, turned himself into the world's Number One wine travel guide, leading enthusiasts to the vineyards of Russia, China, and who knows where next? For several generations, various Wiles have served up rum omelette soufflés on Sunday mornings, thereby providing, we're sure, the right inspiration for just such achievement!

We imagine here a rather late breakfast – not quite a brunch – with Sunday papers spread, bacon and all that sort of frippery if you choose, plus *watergruwel*, which we find, frankly, bizarre. Wondering when to eat this concoction of barley, dried fruits, and red currant juice, we decided we liked it best, chilled, for breakfast – and we *do* like it! Another Dutch recipe from Richard Wiersum – the Dutch being great consumers of barley – it's vaguely like Bircher muesli and has a ripe quality that soothes and refreshes.

Make the toast for this elevenses from Sally Lunn, a kind of very light brioche whose name is either a corruption of *soleil lune* (sun and moon), a type of French breakfast cake, or that of an eighteenth-century Bath baker who reputedly hawked her goods round that English city. With this, a clear amber quince jelly, plus an intriguing preserve based on vegetable marrow.

Preparation is a cinch, provided you've put up preserves and jelly in their respective seasons. Make Sally Lunns either in advance and freeze them, or the day before and eat them fresh. Do the *watergruwel* a day or two ahead, and then all that's left is to whisk the omelette.

AWS

132

It would be a daring host who did not offer coffee and tea at breakfast, though few of us have the panache of Dr. Lou Skinner of our Miami, Florida Society who once presented me with 27 varieties of tea from which to choose.

You may feel, however, that the sophistication of this far-from-*petit déjeuner* warrants one of the various mixtures of champagne and orange juice. Terms for this have been so misquoted that I asked permission of Patrick Forbes, author of perhaps the finest book on champagne since that of the Victorian wine writer Henry Vizitelly, to reproduce his definitive statement:

> In 1921, the barman of Buck's Club in London, Mr. McGarry, invented a delicious pre-luncheon drink, composed of one-third orange juice, two-thirds champagne and a teaspoonful of grenadine, which came to be known as Buck's Fizz; at the Ritz Bar in Paris a mixture of one-third orange juice and two-thirds champagne is served without the grenadine, and is called a Mimosa; at the Carlton Hotel in Cannes a somewhat similar cocktail, made with one-third orange juice, one-third champagne and one-third cognac plus two dashes each of grenadine and cointreau, is known as a Pick-me-up.

Perhaps if the previous night's dinner was a heavy one, the latter mixture might be most advisable before tackling the Wile family omelette.

HD-M

Rum omelette soufflé

The recipe seems to us ample for four, and not *two* people as specified by Julius – but the Wiles admit they owe to it their health and longevity, so perhaps large helpings *are* the answer. Start then by making one of these, and if not enough, follow with another.

4 large or 6 small eggs
15 g/½ oz butter

One 15-ml spoon/1 tbs icing
(confectioners') sugar
45 ml/3 tbs Jamaica rum

Slowly heat an omelette or good, heavy frying pan of 25–30 cm/ 10–12 in diameter to a moderate temperature while separating the eggs, beating the whites until stiff, and whisking the yolks to break them up. Deftly fold together whites and yolks until just combined, melt the butter to coat bottom and sides of the pan, turn the heat beneath it to medium low and pour in the egg mixture. Carefully level the eggs with a spatula.

Cook gently for 10–15 minutes until golden on the bottom and puffed to a height of 4–5 cm/1½–2 inches. In the meantime, warm the rum.

Loosen the sides of the omelette and slide it onto a warm serving plate, folding it in half as you go. Sieve over the icing or confectioners' sugar, ignite and pour on the rum, basting until the flames die out.

Dash to the table and serve the omelette immediately; the result is moist and light and cannot be kept waiting.

For a drier, more stable version, finish the omelette off in a 205°C/400°F/gas mark 6 oven for a minute or two – provided your pan has an ovenproof handle – before slipping it onto its plate.

Julius Wile, New York Wine & Food Society, USA

Watergruwel

For the red currant aspect, we used German "red currant nectar" – *bessensap* in Dutch – from a London supermarket, and we recommend strewing the surface of the *watergruwel* with grape-nuts or similar cereal to add texture when serving.

120 g/4 oz barley groats – brown ones, not white "pearl"
1 litre/35 fl oz/4½ cups water
90 g/3 oz dried currants

120 g/4 oz raisins
About 240 ml/8 fl oz/1 cup red currant juice or "nectar"
Grape-nuts or other crunchy cereal

Soak the barley for 2 hours. Drain and rinse it and cover it with the water. Bring this slowly to the boil and simmer for 20 minutes, stirring occasionally. Add the currants, raisins, and red currant juice, bring back to the boil, and simmer for a further 10 minutes, when the barley should be tender. There will not be much liquid left at this stage; add a drop more juice or a little water if you think it best.

Turn the *watergruwel* into a decorative bowl, cool it, and chill overnight. Serve sprinkled with cereal to give some contrasting crunch.

Richard Wiersum, Surrey, England

Sally Lunn

Sally Lunn crossed the Atlantic to become a popular recipe in the colonies of 18th-century America. This amount makes three round loaves; use one or two of them for breakfast here and freeze the remainder, or turn one into the chocolate dessert on page 213. In some people's versions, thick cream replaces butter.

240 ml/8 fl oz/1 cup milk
90 g/3 oz/just less than ½ cup
  granulated sugar
2–2½ × 5-ml spoons/2–2½ teasp
  salt, depending on whether
  salted or unsalted butter is used
120 g/4 oz butter, unsalted if
  possible

30 g/1 oz fresh yeast or dry yeast
  of equivalent potential
3 eggs
600 g/20 oz/4 cups strong plain
  white or unbleached flour; or
  all-purpose flour (USA); or
  cake flour (South Africa)
1 egg yolk
Butter for toast

Using a jam thermometer as guide, heat the milk, sugar, salt, and butter in a saucepan to a temperature of 49°C/120°F, whisking to dissolve the seasonings and melt the butter. Pour into a large mixing bowl.

Liquefy the yeast in a little warm water, beat the eggs, and stir both ingredients into the milk.

Sift the flour, and by hand, beat 450 g/15 oz/3 cups of it into the bowl until all is well-blended. Add the remaining flour and beat by hand for 5 minutes, turning the bowl and constantly bringing the dough in from the sides. It is a soft, sticky batter which, with beating, becomes very elastic. Scrape the sides of the bowl, cover the top with a plastic sheet and weight this with a bread board. Set aside in a cool place for several hours until the dough has tripled in bulk.

Butter the interiors of three 900 ml/1½ pint/4 cup Parisian *brioche* tins – these are the round, fluted tins which we think of as the classic *brioche* shape – or high round cake tins of equivalent capacity. Punch down the dough, divide it into three equal portions – difficult, as it is tenaciously elastic – and drop each portion into a tin. Smooth and round the tops, cover them with a cloth, and let the dough rise in a cool room for an additional hour or two until blooming over the sides of the tins.

Brush each cake carefully with the egg yolk beaten in a little water. Put two of them into the centre of a 190°C/375°F/gas mark 5 oven. After 15 minutes, lower the heat to 180°C/350°F/gas mark 4, and then keep an eye on the loaves, as the tops burn easily. Cover them with foil, if necessary, to prevent this.

After cakes have baked 30–35 minutes at the lower temperature, test them with a trussing needle thrust into one of the centres. If the needle emerges very hot, the Sally Lunns are done. If not, bake a bit longer. Then turn out the loaves, invert them onto a heavy baking sheet and return them to the oven for 5 minutes to crisp the bottoms. Cool right sides up on a cake rack. Repeat the process with the third Sally Lunn.

When the loaves are cold, freeze what you're not about to use, well-wrapped, and in due course slice the rest about 1½ cm/½ in thick to make toast. Butter well, and serve hot with jams and preserves, for which two suggestions follow.

Marrow lemon preserve

By "marrow" we mean the large green-striped member of the gourd family which is big brother to courgettes (zucchini). Marrows are a gardener's glut in the late English summer, and many recipes – often desperate – have been devised to use up some of the quantity. One such is marrow and ginger jam, of which there are almost as many versions as there are British gardening cooks, but this preserve – related to lemon curd – is more unusual. Its texture resembles a light and crunchy apple sauce, but the taste is pure lemon.

People in non-marrow countries should substitute a hard-rinded gourd or squash with very firm flesh.

1 very large, firm vegetable marrow, or equivalent, or 2 smaller ones, to yield 720 g/1½ lb flesh after seeding and peeling
360 g/12 oz/1¾ cups granulated or preserving sugar

90 g/3 oz butter, preferably without salt
Pinch of salt, if butter is unsalted
2 large lemons

Halve the marrow across the middle, halve each half lengthwise, scoop out and discard the seeds, and with a sharp knife pare off the rind.

Cut the flesh into 1½ cm/½ in dice and steam these – in several batches – over boiling water, until soft and translucent. Each batch will take about 20 minutes.

Drain the marrow very well and purée it in the food processor – just enough to take care of all lumps but not to make it ultra smooth.

Transfer this to a stainless steel or lined copper saucepan, add sugar, butter, salt if required, and the grated zest and strained juice of both lemons. Bring to the boil and simmer gently for 20 minutes, stirring occasionally to prevent sticking. Pot the preserve without delay into hot, dry, sterilised jam jars and cover immediately.

Makes three small pots.

Quince jelly

Crab-apples or medlars can be used instead.

2½ kg/5 lb hard quinces
Sugar – preserving if available, otherwise granulated

Vanilla bean
Lemons

Wash the quinces and cut them up coarsely, retaining peel, seeds, and cores. Put all into two large saucepans, cover with water, bring water to the boil, and simmer for about an hour, until the fruit is *very* soft.

Make up a jelly bag with four layers of muslin or cheesecloth washed and wrung out and tied to the four legs of a high, upturned stool. Put a large bowl well below the bag. Or, wet and wring out a proper jelly bag and suspend it high above the bowl – we hang ours from a drying rack over the bathtub, with the bowl in the bath!

Pour quinces and their cooking liquid into the bag and let the juice drip into the bowl, overnight and undisturbed, without pressing or squeezing fruit or bag.

The next day, measure the juice into a preserving pan or stainless steel saucepan, and for every 600 ml/1 pint/2½ cups of juice, add 480 g/1 lb/a generous 2⅓ cups sugar and the pared zest and strained juice of a lemon. Dissolve sugar in the quince juice over a low heat, split the vanilla bean, tie it up in a little muslin or cheesecloth bag and add to the mixture. Boil briskly until jelly reaches the setting point – 105°C/220°F on a jam thermometer – which can take up to 15 minutes or more. Test for setting before proceeding.

Off the heat, remove the surface froth, the vanilla and the lemon zest, and pot the jelly immediately into hot, dry, sterilised jam jars. Cover them fast.

Makes 2–3 jars.

A copious picnic
for eight

AYRAN
Frothy yoghurt drink

AYAM KICHUP LIM
Spiced chicken

BOILED PICKLED OX TONGUE, SAUCE GRIBICHE

BARBECUED SWEETBREADS AND ONIONS

HAVUÇ TARATOR
Carrot and yoghurt salad

BLACK MUSHROOMS

CHOCOLATE-HAZELNUT TORTE

BUTTERSCOTCH COOKIES

FRESH FRUIT

A copious picnic
for eight

This is a truly international and rather garlicky spread. We've contributed a Turkish drink and salad, plus some mushrooms cooked way down in red wine till they turn black – a hit with garlic-loving children. From Hiang Holtom, *née* Lim, we have Malaysian chicken drumsticks, stuffed and subtly spiced; from Dorothy Gibson of Melbourne, widow of our former President Victor Gibson, a pickled ox tongue to which we've added some sharp sauce; from America a European cake, and then dozens of Midwestern butterscotch cookies via Elizabeth Charpie of Boston.

Barbecue fiends should have great fun with Frank Lloyd Wright's ingenuous sweetbreads and onions, the onions cooked under "any brand" of coffee can, to quote the contributor.

Alternatives for barbecuing are salmon in a beer and soy sauce marinade, page 192, from Stanley Oleksiuk, one of our gastronomic doctors, or parcels of chicken in honey, soy, and sesame sauce, page 198, which would replace Hiang Holtom's spiced chicken or the Oleksiuk salmon but not accompany them. As a change from the black mushrooms, there are Audrey Wilkerson's sweet-sour beans, page 211.

It's a picnic, so *everything* gets done in advance, in your own time, except for the barbecue.

AWS

The devotees of *ayram* will probably stay with it throughout. I can't stand it myself.

If you are taking a white or rosé wine, chill it a little more than usual.

Then either transport the bottles in an insulated carrier, or simply wrap them well in Turkish towelling.

It is wise to take some soft drinks, plus a large thermos full of ice cubes. When freezing these for a picnic, I drop a cherry or a small wedge of pineapple into each niche of the trays, with the water. Decorative and fun. If you squirt a little soda water into the thermos on top of the cubes, it helps prevent them from fusing together.

HD-M

Ayran

A Turkish drink – made there from sheep's milk yoghurt – that's cool and uplifting in the heat. You find it all over the country, in homes and restaurants and carried through city streets by small boys crying *ayran! ayran!* Not all your picnickers will want it, but those who do tend to drink it in quantity. Enough for 8 people, or 4 fanatics.

1200 ml/2 pints/5 cups plain yoghurt, half each goats'/ewes' and cows' milk, if possible

About 750 ml/1¼ pints/3 cups cold water; perhaps a bit less
Salt

Beat or blend the water into the yoghurt, with gusto, add salt to taste, and beat again; *ayran* should be frothy. Chill well, transport in thermos flasks.

Ayam kichup Lim

Messy to eat, but delicious. Serve 1 leg per person, with plenty of napkins.

8 chicken legs, thigh and drumstick
   in one piece

Stuffing
2 fillets of chicken breast
1 large onion
150 g/5 oz mushrooms
One 5-ml spoon/1 teasp ground or
   well-crushed coriander seeds

One 2.5-ml spoon/½ teasp
   cornflour (cornstarch)
Salt and pepper

To finish
Oil for deep-frying, plus 75 ml/5
   tbs peanut oil for sauce
3 large cloves garlic
3 medium onions
1½ × 15-ml spoons/1½ tbs each
   roasted, ground peanuts and
   concentrated tomato paste
1 heaped 1.25-ml spoon/¼ heaped
   teasp dried lemongrass (available
   from Chinese supermarkets)

1 scant 2.5-ml spoon/½ scant teasp
   ground turmeric
A pinch grated nutmeg
1½ × 5-ml spoons/1½ teasp
   granulated sugar
One 2.5-ml spoon/½ teasp
   cornflour (cornstarch)
Juice of ½ a large lemon
Salt and pepper

Bone the legs, leaving their trimmed, bulbous ends intact; turn them skin side out.

To make the stuffing, finely chop the chicken breasts, peeled onion, and well-washed mushrooms, mix them with coriander, cornflour (cornstarch), salt and pepper. With wet hands, stuff the mixture into the drumstick part of each leg, fold the flap of thigh skin neatly over the filling, round each form to give it a good shape, and secure the loose skin with a small poultry skewer.

Heat the oil for deep frying so it is hot but not smoking and fry the stuffed legs, two or three at a time, until golden and crispy. Carefully remove their skewers and set the chicken aside on kitchen paper that will absorb excess oil.

Peel the garlic and remaining onions, chop them coarsely and whiz to a paste – with the help of a little oil – in the food processor or blender. Heat the peanut oil in a large sauté pan, put in the onion-garlic paste and fry until it browns slightly. Add the ground peanuts, tomato paste, lemongrass, turmeric, nutmeg, sugar, and the cornflour (cornstarch) diluted in the lemon juice. Season the sauce with salt and pepper, let it simmer for a few minutes to cook the cornflour.

Put the chicken into a shallow baking dish, coat it with the sauce and bake at 180°C/350°F/gas mark 4 for about 15 minutes.

Transport the sauced chicken in a clean, well-wrapped baking dish or lidded plastic box to the picnic site.

Hiang Holtom, South Bank branch, London, England

Boiled pickled ox tongue

If pickled tongue is not available, fresh beef tongue may of course be substituted.

One 1200–1400 g/2½–3 lb pickled ox tongue	1 bay leaf
	Salt, if tongue has not been pickled
30 ml/2 tbs vinegar	
One 15-ml spoon/1 tbs brown sugar	6 black peppercorns

Scrub the tongue well, put it into a large, heavy pot of cold water to cover, bring water slowly to the boil, and skim thoroughly. Simmer for 10 minutes; if the water tastes very salty, throw it away, plunge the tongue into cold water, drain it after a few minutes, and lower it into a second pot of simmering water. Add vinegar, sugar, and bay leaf. (If the tongue is fresh, omit the blanching, and add salt to seasonings just listed). Simmer the tongue, ¾-covered, over a low heat for 2½–3 hours – adding peppercorns during the last stages of cooking, and skimming periodically – until a skewer pierces the meat easily.

Remove the pot from the heat and the tongue from its broth and cool it just enough to handle. Remove roots, small neck bones, and gristle from the tongue's base, skin and trim it and return it to the cooking liquid to cool completely. Skinning is much easier at this stage than later.

When the meat is cold, extract it from the broth – which from a pickled tongue will probably be too salty to use as a stock for soup – dry it, wrap well in foil, and chill it overnight. Slice at the picnic – or at home if easier – and serve with a *sauce gribiche*, as follows.

Dorothy Gibson, The Ladies Wine & Food Society of Melbourne, Australia

Sauce gribiche

450 ml/¾ pint/2 cups basic
  vinaigrette, page 221, but
  without the garlic
3 hard-boiled eggs
2 shallots
One 5-ml spoon/1 teasp capers

4 or 5 small pickled cucumbers or
  gherkins
Two 15-ml spoons/2 tbs chopped
  fresh herbs, such as parsley,
  tarragon, chives, chervil
Salt and pepper

Make the vinaigrette, peel and finely-chop the eggs and shallots, dry and chop the capers and pickles. Mix these into the vinaigrette with the herbs, and season to taste. Transport the sauce in a leak-proof container and shake well before serving with the tongue.

Barbecued sweetbreads and onions

These days, our only chance to barbecue comes as occasional guests of an expert – but we were intrigued and amused by the following two recipes from Frank Lloyd Wright which we give those of you who barbecue more or less verbatim, as alternatives or supplements to everything else.

Sweetbreads

4 pairs very fresh veal sweetbreads,
  soaked for 3–4 hours in several
  changes of cold water to purge
  of blood and impurities
1 part olive oil

5 parts dry white or red wine
Fresh parsley and basil
Peeled, crushed garlic
Salt and pepper

Do nothing to sweetbreads except possibly butterfly larger ones. Place directly on grill; a good, deep bed of coals, without flames, is essential, and heat must be maintained for at least an hour. During cooking, brush sweetbreads frequently with a baste made of the other seven ingredients, well stirred to integrate wine and oil. Don't be disturbed by flames that flare when the sweetbreads are moistened.

They should be barbecued slowly, and when properly done, will be firm and golden outside and juicy within. Cooking should last about an hour, give or take a few minutes; when ready, simply cut to bite size and serve hot.

Onions

8 large onions, red if possible
Enough 480 g/1 lb or larger metal
   coffee cans – "any brand" – to
   cover all the onions

Melted butter
Salt and pepper

Have a good, deep, flameless bed of coals whose heat can be maintained for at least 50 minutes.

Do nothing to onions. Place them directly on grill and cover with cans. In about 20 minutes, lift covers, turn onions over, and replace cans. After another 20 minutes, decide if onions are done, remove them if so – cook longer if not – trim both ends, and peel off skins. Cut up the flesh, coat with butter, grind on seasoning, and serve.

Frank Lloyd Wright Jr., Washington, D.C. Wine & Food Society,
USA

Havuç tarator

A Turkish salad of yoghurt and carrots whose elusive flavour derives from *tahini*, or sesame paste, available from specialist grocers. In Turkey, as for *ayran*, the yoghurt would be made from ewes' milk. We're grateful to Muktar Yusuf, proprietor of The Golden Horn Restaurant in London, for parting with the secrets of this recipe.

1 litre/35 fl oz/4½ cups plain
   yoghurt
2–2½ × 15-ml spoons/2–2½ tbs
   tahini paste
360 g/12 oz carrots, weighed after
   peeling and trimming

2–3 large cloves garlic
Salt
20–30 ml/1½–2 tbs lemon juice
A small handful of chopped parsley
Pepper

Drain the yoghurt overnight in cheesecloth or muslin to be rid of excess water, then whisk in the *tahini*. Use the blender here, if necessary, to integrate thoroughly.

Prepare the carrots and finely shred half of them. This is easily done in the food processor fitted with the shredding disk. Boil the other half in salted water for 5 minutes, drain, dry well and shred as above. Mix all carrots into the yoghurt, peel and crush the garlic to a purée with some salt, add it together with the lemon juice, parsley, pepper, and additional salt to the yoghurt base. Check the seasoning – the *tahini* should be subtle – and chill for several hours.

Carry to the picnic in a tightly-lidded plastic box.

Black mushrooms

1400 g/3 lb button mushrooms	*Shallots*
Olive oil	*Garlic*
Salt	*Parsley*
Fruity red wine	*Pepper*
Basic vinaigrette, page 221	

Halve or quarter the mushrooms, wash them thoroughly, heat a little oil in one or two large heavy saucepans and begin to sauté them, stirring several times, for a few minutes. Add a little salt and enough red wine just to cover, and simmer the mushrooms without lids until the wine has almost evaporated.

Off the heat, toss the fungi – whose volume will have greatly reduced – with a little vinaigrette while they are still hot. When all is cool, drain away the excess dressing and season the salad with a lot of finely-chopped shallots, garlic, parsley, salt, and pepper. This is a dish which we always make by "sight" and taste, and it's difficult to give exact quantities for ingredients; the result should be highly piquant. Transport to the picnic as for the *havuç tarator*.

Chocolate-hazelnut torte

Torte

Fine dry bread or cake crumbs	*150 g/5 oz/¾ cup castor*
150 g/5oz softened butter,	*(granulated) sugar*
unsalted if possible	*6 eggs, separated*

150 g/5 oz semi-sweet chocolate   180 g/6 oz toasted and ground
                                           hazel-nuts

Icing
150 g/5 oz butter, unsalted if   2 eggs
  possible, and softened   150 g/5 oz semi-sweet chocolate
60 g/4 tbs castor (granulated)
  sugar

To finish
30 ml/2 tbs dark rum   45–60 g/3–4 tbs raspberry jam

Butter a 20–23 cm/8–9 in spring-form cake tin, line the bottom with a
circle of buttered greaseproof or parchment paper, and dust the tin with
bread or cake crumbs.

To make the torte, cream 120 g/4 oz of the butter until soft, gradually
beat in the sugar and beaten egg yolks. Break up the chocolate and melt
it, with the remaining 30 g/1 oz butter, in a heavy saucepan which
should be set, covered, inside a larger pan of just-boiled water. Whisk
smooth, cool slightly, and beat into the butter base. Stir in the nuts.

Whisk the egg whites until stiff, beat $\frac{1}{3}$ of them into the base to
lighten it, then deftly fold this into the remaining whites. Quickly pour
the torte mixture into the spring-form pan and bake at 180°C/350°F/gas
mark 4 for 30–40 minutes before removing it to a wire rack and cooling
completely. Spring cake from tin, peel paper from its base and
refrigerate overnight.

To make the icing, cream together 120 g/4 oz of the softened butter,
the sugar, and eggs. Melt the chocolate and the remaining 30 g/1 oz
butter as above, whisk smooth, cool slightly, and beat this into the
butter base.

Remove the torte from the refrigerator and cut it in half horizontally
with a serrated knife. Dilute the rum with a little water and with a pastry
brush imbibe the cut side of each half with this mixture. Spread the
raspberry jam over the cut side of the lower half and cover with a third of
the icing. Sandwich with the other cut side, and spread the whole cake
with the rest of the icing, swirling it into an attractive pattern.

The torte can be refrigerated, covered, for up to a week, and carried
carefully to the picnic.

Barbara D. Holland, Columbus, Ohio Wine & Food Society, USA

Butterscotch cookies

A recipe handed along to Beth Charpie by her grandmother, who learned it in the 1850s as a girl in Ohio. It makes a vast amount of dough that is shaped into rolled loaves to be frozen, then baked as needed.

480 g/1 lb softened butter,
  preferably unsalted
960 g/2 lb/a generous 5 cups light
  brown sugar
15 ml/1 tbs vanilla extract
4 eggs

900–1000 g/30–35 oz/6–7 cups
  plain flour
Two 5-ml spoons/2 teasp each
  baking soda and cream of tartar
One 5-ml spoon/1 teasp salt

Cream the butter, gradually beat in the sugar, vanilla extract, and the whisked eggs.

Sift together the smaller amount (900 g/30 oz/6 cups) of flour, the baking soda, cream of tartar, and salt; beat this into the butter base and add enough extra flour, sifted, to enable you to form the dough into four rolls of about 5–6½ cm/2–2½ in diameter by 25 cm/10 in long.

Wrap each roll in foil and then plastic wrap and freeze what you don't want to use right away. The frozen rolls can be kept for months and sliced with a sharp knife into cookies which are baked from frozen.

Refrigerate the roll(s) for immediate use until firm, then cut each into ¾ cm/¼ in disks. Bake these on heavy, ungreased baking sheets for about 15 minutes at 165°C/325°F/gas mark 3. Cool the cookies on racks and store them in tins.

Each roll makes 40 cookies.

Elizabeth Charpie, Boston Wine & Food Society, USA

Cocktail parties

CANAPÉS WITH WATERCRESS, STILTON,
AND CURRIED LIME BUTTERS

CHEDDAR TURNOVERS

ÇIĞ KÖFTE
Lamb and pepper rissoles

MOUTHFULS OF CORN

SQUID STICKS

CARROT AND POPPY TARTLETS

ARTICHOKE BOATS

PARMESAN BACON

CIRCASSIAN VEGETABLES

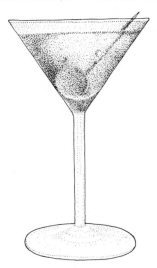

Cocktail parties

Cocktails from 5 to 7 – or 6 to 8 – or even later, depending on your country – will always recur, whether indoors, outside, gloriously catered, or hurriedly based on some salted peanuts.

As for cocktail food, the best I know would be platefuls of American gastronome James Beard's tiny sandwiches of onion set between circles of brioche, the edges then rolled in mayonnaise and chopped parsley to form a heavy encircling wreath. Sheer heaven.

For those who are hungrier, a few suggestions for additional mouthfuls: circles of toast with three whipped butters, cheese turnovers in rich cheese pastry, and two more ideas from the Turkish repertoire – one for a fiery street food based on raw lamb and *burghul*, the other a famous chicken dish in bite-size version.

From Pamela Vandyke Price there are crunchy fingers of corn, and from Jack Witter, our squid expert, chilied and fried squid sticks – fiddly to make but deliciously crisp and not served everywhere. Then tiny, two-bite quiches of shredded carrots and a sprinkling of poppy seeds, artichoke bottoms piled with spinach, ham, and horseradish, and easiest of all, a "savoury" of bacon tossed in Parmesan cheese and quickly grilled.

There are nine ideas for you to choose from, a few variations, hot things and cold, some complete in advance, others wanting last-minute care. Remember that people tend to eat more when drinking what I once called "liquor drinks" than when concentrating on wine, mineral water, or fruit juice.

AWS

Commander Anthony Hogg, one of our "professionals", retired from a distinguished career in the wine trade and shortly produced *Cocktails and Mixed Drinks,* * a definitive book on cocktails. His friend André Simon might not have approved, having once written: "Cocktails are an abomination. . . They paralyse the taste buds and fog the brain so that any fine cooking or fine wine has absolutely no chance of being appreciated". Surprisingly, however, André's famous *Encyclopædia of Gastronomy* contains no less than 92 recipes for exactly these poisons!

Though the Commander's book gives a cool 400 possibilities, he does distinguish the "Big Seven", and in my opinion, no self-respecting cocktail host should omit to serve at least one of them. They are as follows: Martini and White Lady (both gin-based), Manhattan (whiskey), Daiquiri (rum), Old Fashioned (whiskey), Sidecar (brandy) and Jack Rose (applejack). Dale Carnegie did not teach his pupils that the best way to Lose Friends and Upset People is to tell them that their proportions for a Dry Martini are all wrong, but he should have done. So we don't intend to trespass on Anthony's part of the ship by giving you his formulae, but we do propose that you offer a few additional choices. First, a good sparkler; secondly, a fruit drink. We addicts have tasted and blended them all, but find that none compares with the juice of freshly (note, *freshly*) squeezed oranges. Then, perhaps, a chilled *vin rosé*, and certainly some good fizzing mineral water for those who wouldn't wish to be without it.

HD-M

Canapés with watercress, Stilton, and curried lime butters

About 56 mouthfuls.

14 slices of firm white sandwich bread, cut fairly thin	30 g/1 oz cream cheese
420 g/14 oz butter, softened	60 g/2oz Stilton or similar blue cheese
Lemon juice	Cayenne pepper
Lime juice	Mild curry powder
1 bunch watercress	Salt and pepper

*The Hamlyn Publishing Group, 1979

Allow the sliced bread to go rather stale. With a 4 cm/1½ in circular cutter, cut 4 rounds from each slice, toast both sides and lightly spread each round with a very little softened butter.

Divide the remaining butter into three equal portions. Beat each with a wooden spoon until very light and fluffy. Gradually beat into two of the bases 15 ml/1 tbs or more of lemon juice each; and into the third, 15 ml/1 tbs or more of lime.

Remove stems from half the watercress, wash and dry the leaves, chop them finely and beat these into one of the lemon bases. Taste, and judge whether to chop and add more leaves or to squeeze in more lemon. Season well.

Into the second lemon butter beat the cream cheese and the Stilton or similar blue, worked into a paste, plus a very little cayenne pepper, salt and pepper and more lemon if necessary.

Into the lime butter whip a fair amount of curry powder, plus salt and pepper and extra lime to taste.

These butters can wait, loosely covered with plastic wrap, for several hours in a cool place.

To serve, give all three of them a final whip, pile each into its own small bowl, and serve surrounded by a few appropriately-buttered rounds of toast to get things started, plus the remaining rounds to be prepared and eaten as needed.

Cheddar turnovers

30–40 pieces.
If you can't find Cheddar cheese, use a similar hard and mature variety.

Pastry

420 g/14 oz/a generous 2¾ cups plain flour
A pinch of salt if needed

300 g/10 oz each of firm butter, unsalted if possible, and Cheddar or similar cheese
2 eggs

To finish

About 450 g/15 oz Gruyère, mozzarella, or Cheshire cheese, or a similar type to one of these

2 egg yolks

To make the pastry, sift the flour with salt – if using unsalted butter – dice the butter, and cut or rub it into the flour; grate in the cheese.

Whisk the eggs together and add enough to bind the pastry without making it wet. Wrap it in paper, then put it into a plastic bag and refrigerate for several hours or overnight.

Remove pastry from the refrigerator half an hour before use, roll it out on a floured board in 2–3 rounds of $\frac{1}{2}$ cm/$\frac{1}{8}$ in thick, and cut out circles of about 6 cm/2$\frac{1}{4}$ in diameter.

Mound some thinly-sliced Gruyère or other cheese slightly off the centre of each round, brush pastry borders with a little of the egg yolks beaten in a dash of water, and fold the pastry over to make a fairly compact turnover, pressing edges together with the tines of a fork. Trim the edges, knock them up with the back of a knife, and brush tops with the egg wash.

Re-roll the off-cuts and use all the dough. It softens quickly, so don't let it get too warm as you work.

Refrigerate turnovers for at least half an hour – overnight if you like, lightly covered with foil – then bake them at 190°C/375°F/gas mark 5 for about 20 minutes until the pastry is cooked through and has turned a warm, golden, cheesy colour. Serve hot.

These re-heat perfectly – 190°C/375°F/gas mark 5 for 10 minutes – and are rich and fragile.

Çiğ köfte

About 60 rissoles.

At Van, an Eastern Turkish town that was once a part of Armenia, we found much excellent street food, the best of which were çiğ köfte. Three men in different parts of the market quarter stood kneading raw minced lamb with *burghul* or cracked wheat (explained on page 18), tomatoes, hot pepper, and other ingredients, working the mixture on round brass trays and breaking off bits – rolled into balls and then in parsley – for us to taste. They were fiery but delicious, a little like steak tartare and not dissimilar to the Lebanese *kibbeh*. This recipe goes easier on the chili than any of those we sampled.

480 g/16 oz lamb shoulder, boned
    weight
60 g/2 oz fine burghul, available
    from natural food stores and
    Middle Eastern grocers
1$\frac{1}{2}$ fresh chili peppers

60 g/2 oz onion, peeled weight
A very large bunch of very fresh
    parsley
240 g/8 oz fresh, ripe tomatoes
Salt
Cayenne pepper

Separate the meat into muscles and carefully cut away all fat, membranes, and connective tissue, leaving about 240 g/8 oz of meat. Meanwhile soak the *burghul* in very hot water, to cover, for 20 minutes or until tender.

Grind the lamb till very smooth in a meat grinder or food processor. Squeeze the *burghul* of excess moisture, let it cool, and knead together the two ingredients.

Seed the chilis and mince them with the onion in a food processor, or chop both very fine. Peel, seed, and chop the tomatoes. Take a handful of the parsley, remove the stems, and chop it.

On a large board, knead all these ingredients gradually into the lamb and *burghul*, add salt and a little cayenne to taste, and with wet hands knead the mixture for 10 minutes.

Scoop the whole thing into a bowl and leave it in a cool place – covered – for several hours or overnight, to mature. The peppers make the meat digestible.

To serve, roll the mixture into balls the size of the first joint of a woman's little finger and roll these in parsley, not too finely chopped.

Mouthfuls of corn

20–30 pieces.

Pamela Vandyke Price uses this mixture to make both a soufflé and a cross between a quiche and tortilla that's baked in a shallow dish. This is the second version. The crunch of fresh corn is an agreeable surprise; at a pinch, frozen or tinned corn can be used, but the result is not comparable.

3–4 ears of fresh young corn, enough to yield 360 g/12 oz of kernels
60 g/2 oz coarse brown breadcrumbs, freshly-made
4 large eggs
210 ml/7 fl oz/⅞ cup milk

30 g/1 oz grated Parmesan cheese
90 g/3 oz grated Gruyère or Emmenthal cheese, or nearest equivalent
Salt and pepper
30 g/1 oz butter

Pull the husks and silk from corn ears and boil them rapidly in unsalted water for 2–4 minutes, until the kernels are tender. Drain the ears well and cut off the kernels, not too deeply, with a small, sharp knife. Toast the breadcrumbs in a low oven until they are crisp.

Whisk together the eggs, milk, corn, and cheeses, add salt and pepper to taste. Butter a 25 cm/10 in quiche dish, or other shallow baking dish with right-angle sides, spread it with half the corn mixture, then half the crumbs, followed by the remaining egg and corn and the second lot of crumbs. Dot with the 30 g/1 oz butter cut into chips.

Bake for 25 minutes at 190°C/375°F/gas mark 5, until the top rises, the crumbs brown further and the butter sizzles.

Serve warm, cut into small, slim wedges. If you make this in advance, reheat it uncut at the above temperature for 8–10 minutes.

Pamela Vandyke Price, London, England

Squid sticks

2 large squid, fresh or frozen,	Flour
weighing about 450 g/15 oz	Chili powder
each, or smaller squid of	Salt
equivalent total weight	Oil for deep-frying

Prepare and trim the squid as described in the recipe for squid Chinese-style on page 126, using the tentacles and trimmings for some other purpose, like the basis of a broth or stuffing.

Open the skinned squid pouches, pull away their mucous membranes and cut the squid into strips of about $\frac{3}{4} \times 8$ cm/$\frac{1}{4} \times 3$ in. Lay the strips on baking sheets and dry them in a 115°C/240°F/gas mark $\frac{1}{4}$ oven for 20–30 minutes.

Sift together some flour, a little chili powder, and some salt onto a plate. Toss a small quantity of the sticks in this, shake off the excess, and deep-fry the squid in hot oil until crisp. Drain on kitchen paper, salt, and serve.

It's best, if you can, to do the final flouring, frying, and salting in small batches, served quickly, rather than frying all the sticks at once, as the results will have a fresher crunch.

J. A. Witter, New South Wales Wine & Food Society, Australia

Carrot and poppy tartlets

30 pieces.

About 210 g/7 oz of shortcrust I,   *15 g/½ oz butter*
   page 222   *Salt and pepper*
2 medium carrots, enough to yield   *1 large egg*
   60 g/2 oz when shredded   *30 ml/2 tbs cream*
2 shallots   *Poppy seeds*

Roll out the pastry thinly and line 30 round metal tartlet moulds of 4 cm/1½ in diameter. Use any leftover pastry for something else, and refrigerate the shells for half an hour.

Place tiny pieces of greaseproof or parchment paper weighted with rice or dried beans inside each tin and cook the shells on heavy baking sheets at 165°C/325°F/gas mark 3 for 10 or 15 minutes until the pastry has set and is just beginning to colour. Remove from the oven and cool the shells slightly before flipping them out of the moulds and returning them to the baking sheets.

Meanwhile, scrape, trim, and finely shred the carrots (shredding disk of the food processor does this in seconds), peel and mince the shallots. Melt the butter in a small, heavy saucepan and sweat the vegetables, covered, for 5 minutes or so, until the carrots have just cooked. Season them. Whisk together the egg and cream, add salt and pepper.

The three components of these tartlets can be prepared in advance and assembled at the last minute for final baking.

Put a little carrot and shallot into each shell, sprinkle with a few poppy seeds and spoon on some of the egg and cream.

Bake for about 15 minutes in a 180°C/350°F/gas mark 4 oven until the tops have swelled and begun to colour. Serve warm.

Artichoke boats

30 pieces.

A modification of a recipe long used by Alice's mother.

15 artichoke bottoms, in oil or
   brine, plus a few extra in case
   of mishaps
10–12 fresh young spinach leaves
60 g/2 oz thinly-sliced boiled ham

45 g/1½ oz cooked and shelled
   shrimp or prawns
Grated horseradish
Mayonnaise
Salt and pepper

Drain the artichoke bottoms, pat them dry, trim away all rough and spiky edges and cut each in half across the centre to form a vaguely boat-like shape.

Remove stems from the spinach, wash and dry it well, and finely chop the leaves. Cut the ham into slivers and the slivers into dice. Dry and chop the shrimps.

Put all of these into a bowl, with any spike-less artichoke trimmings, well-chopped, add some grated horseradish and enough mayonnaise to bind without making the mixture runny.

Season to taste – horseradish should be evident but not overpowering – and pile the mixture onto each boat.

Don't make these up too far ahead. If necessary, keep them in the refrigerator, under a cover which doesn't touch, until shortly before serving.

Parmesan bacon

64 pieces.

A between-the-Wars British savoury, served then as an after-dinner digestive, adapted here to pre-dinner drinks.

8 thin slices streaky (belly) bacon,
   unsmoked

A handful of fine, dry
   breadcrumbs
Grated Parmesan cheese

Remove rinds, if present, from the bacon slices, cut each into half lengthwise, and each half into four pieces.

Strew the breadcrumbs on a plate, mix in enough grated Parmesan to suggest its flavour, and toss the bacon pieces – about 10 at a time – in the mixture. A fine coating of crumbs will adhere.

Slowly grill (broil) the bacon pieces about 2–3 minutes on each side until they sizzle and become crisp. Serve immediately.

Circassian vegetables

20 pieces.

Circassian chicken is a Turkish dish of poached chicken in a walnut sauce, dribbled with oil and paprika. Here, the chicken is folded into the sauce and used as a stuffing for tomatoes and mushrooms.

20 little cherry tomatoes, or
20 tiny button mushrooms, very fresh and white and no more than 2 cm/¾ in across or a combination of these
The juice of a lemon
120 g/4 oz cooked chicken meat (about the value of one large chicken breast, wing attached)
150 ml/5 fl oz/scant ⅔ cup chicken broth, made by poaching the

above breast in water with a little sliced carrot and onion and salt
45 g/1½ oz finely-ground walnuts
15 g/½ oz fresh breadcrumbs, brown if possible
A small clove of garlic
Salt and pepper
One 1.25-ml spoon/¼ teasp paprika
7 ml/½ tbs oil – walnut if possible

Cut the tops from the tomatoes and scoop out their innards with the handle of a small spoon. Remove stems from the mushrooms, wipe them well with a damp cloth and hold them in a bowl, covered with lemon juice.

Poach the chicken in salted water with the onion and carrot for about 10 minutes until cooked, let it cool in the broth, strain and reserve the liquid. Discard the chicken's skin and cut flesh into fine shreds.

Grind the walnuts, make the breadcrumbs, peel and crush the garlic clove. Put 150 ml/5 fl oz/a scant ⅔ cup of the strained broth into a small saucepan and to this add the nuts, breadcrumbs, and garlic. Bring this to the boil and stir briefly until it thickens. Let cool, fold in the chicken, and add salt and pepper to taste. Store this, tightly covered with plastic wrap, in the refrigerator until about half an hour before use. Finally, mix the paprika and oil.

All the above can be done in advance, but leave assembly till you are fairly near to serving the vegetables.

Stuff the tomatoes, pat the mushrooms dry and stuff them, mounding the chicken in either case. Stir the oil and paprika and put a drop onto each piece.

An exotic buffet
for ten

CELERIAC SALAD

COURGETTE FANS, TOMATO, AND MOZZARELLA CHEESE

BOBOTIE
YELLOW RICE WITH RAISINS

SAMBALS AND PLUM CHUTNEY

A PAIR OF BLACK BOTTOM PIES

AUTUMN FRUIT SALAD

An exotic buffet

for ten

The average British buffet is an anything-but-exotic amassing of pâtés, quiches, and cold meats or rather tough-chewing "*bœuf bourguignon*"; not so the South African evening recently organised by Betty Long and Helen Mills, two members of the Surrey Hills branch of the Society. The notable attraction there was a Cape Malay dish called *bobotie* or *bobotje*, escorted by a slightly sweetened rice and a range of condiments known as *sambals*.

Bobotie is a mixture of ground meat or flaked fish and a pungent assortment of spices, some dried fruit like apricots or pears – which give an agreeable grain to the texture – and such details as pumpkin seeds and slivered almonds. The whole is topped by vine leaves if available, bound with egg and milk, and baked. The result is sweet, savoury, and very good. A similar recipe was submitted to us by Mary Furness of London, so things must be looking up for British buffets.

We're told that *bobotie* is perhaps the most popular South African dish of Cape Malay origin, the Malays having come as slaves to the Cape of Good Hope at the end of the seventeenth century. They brought along Eastern spices and an expert knowledge of fishing and cookery which they adapted to local conditions and applied to raw materials like quinces, dried apricots, mackerel, and *snoek* – a fish less alarming than its name and Hitler moustache would indicate.

With *bobotie* and other curried foods, the Malays and their disciples serve small quantities of a large variety of side dishes called *sambals*. Lesley Faull, a friend of André Simon, the author of a considerable list of cookery books, and the founder of a well-known South African cooking school called Silwood Kitchen, says that the basic *sambal*

162

combines fresh chili peppers with onion and garlic crushed together and fried in oil. She details further side dishes, some cooling, some 'hot': grated coconut sautéed in butter till crisp, chopped nuts, balls of paw-paw and sliced bananas sprinkled with lemon juice, preserved ginger, chopped sweet green peppers, quince preserve, diced tomato and onion, fried and chopped bacon, sliced avocado, and many more, including chutney. The usual Cape chutney is based on apricots; we give a plum one from former Chairman George Rainbird that Lesley Faull should find appropriate.

So, make as many *sambals* as the traffic will bear and disperse them along the buffet with Roger Copel's tangy celeriac salad and a platter or two of fanned courgettes with tomatoes, cheese, and a scattering of flowers or leaves. Then bring in the desserts: chocolate mousse in ginger crusts with a lemony cream topping, and a salad of autumn fruits – figs, grapes, plums – simmered in wine and honey. The season? Early October or April, depending on your hemisphere.

A band of graters, choppers, and shredders will be useful to you here. Of course, the chutney will have been made with the plums of late summer, while the *bobotie* can be largely prepared in advance and frozen as described in the recipe.

On the morning of the party, make the celeriac and fruit salads and the black bottom pies. Prepare the courgettes in the afternoon and keep them in their cooking liquid till you're ready to assemble the salad – which should be done fairly near to serving. Tackle *sambals* in the late afternoon. As your guests arrive, bake the *bobotie* and cook the rice.

AWS

South Africans excel at hospitable buffets, as I discovered when I went with a party to visit the Society's members in that country. So it would seem gracious to propose here a variety of their wines. Unfortunately, very few countries sell any South African drink at present, and perhaps the best way to match suitable bottles to this pungent food is to let people choose from a variety of domestic vintages made from the cultivars most widely grown in the Republic. This is an intriguing concept!

The rich steen grape – which accounts for a quarter of the Cape's white wine production – is first cousin to the chenin blanc (or pineau de la Loire), the basis of France's vouvray and anjou white wines. It's found, too, throughout the Californian winelands and even in Israel and Mexico.

South Africa's largest red crop is that of the soft and light cinsau(l)t. Though rarely vinified alone elsewhere, it's the grape that gives roundness to Châteauneuf-du-Pape and to many of the rich bottles of the South of France. But the Republic's best-known red is the distinctive pinotage, a hybrid of pinot noir and hermitage grapes. It hasn't, in my opinion, much resemblance to either, but young wines based on one of them might well be appropriate. The only other country in which I have seen domestic pinotage is New Zealand.

Taste buds savouring the fruit salad would take kindly to the magnificent Edelkeur from Stellenbosch or to one of its cousins-in-rot such as sauternes, German *beerenauslesen*, or the late-harvest rieslings of California. As usual, avoid drinking wine with the chocolate!

HD-M

Celeriac salad

Celeriac – or celery root – discolours fast once peeled and shredded, and needs to be quickly dressed with a sharp sauce.

Four 15-ml spoons/4 tbs French	*180 ml/6 fl oz/¾ cup olive oil*
mustard, Dijon if possible	*120 g/4 oz peeled shallots*
Salt and pepper	*1 kg/2¼ lb celeriac*
90 ml/3 fl oz/generous ⅓ cup wine	*Chopped parsley*
vinegar	

Combine mustard, seasonings, and wine vinegar, slowly whisk in oil. Correct seasoning, which should be assertive.

Mince shallots, peel and quarter celeriac and shred it on a rotary shredder or the shredding disk of a food processor. Immediately toss celeriac with the shallots and dressing until all is well combined, check seasoning, and refrigerate for several hours. Toss again and fleck with parsley to serve.

Roger O. Copel, Northern Illinois Wine & Food Society, USA

Courgette fans, tomato, and mozzarella cheese

In the early autumn, courgettes – zucchini – are still around and haven't all reached marrow-like proportions; or perhaps there are small ones available which have arrived by plane from somewhere. They add to a colourful salad.

½ *bottle dry white wine*
Salt
10 firm courgettes (zucchini), each
  weighing 60–90 g/2–3 oz
8 medium tomatoes, quite ripe
600 g/20 oz mozzarella cheese

2–3 large cloves garlic
Pepper
Olive oil
Fresh marigold petals if still
  available, nasturtium flowers, or
  mint leaves or sorrel

Bring the wine and an equal quantity of water, plus salt, to the boil in a large heavy saucepan. Top and tail courgettes and poach them in two lots, uncovered, in the vinous water, until tender; this takes about 5–7 minutes. Cool, hold till you need them, then drain. The wine will make the flesh quite crisp. (Use the poaching liquid as the basis for soup.)

Have ready one or two large oval platters. Starting 2½–4 cm/1–1½ in from the top of each courgette, slice it lengthways into 4–5 equal sections, spread these into a fan, and pat each fan dry.

Don't peel the tomatoes – I find them infinitely more interesting with the skins, which impart flavour – cut out the woody extension of their stems, and slice thinly from top to bottom. Slice mozzarella, peel and mince garlic.

Arrange the courgettes – nicely fanned – tomato, and cheese in an attractive overlapping fashion on the platter(s), the three colours interlaced. Strew on the chopped garlic, grind on salt and pepper, and dribble over rivulets of olive oil.

Then take fresh marigold petals, if marigolds are still around, plus nasturtium flowers – or small mint leaves – and scatter them over; or take some sorrel leaves, shred them short and fine, and strew on the strips – their crisp acidity is wonderful here. Alternatively, if there's an edible flower, leaf, or herb you prefer, substitute that one.

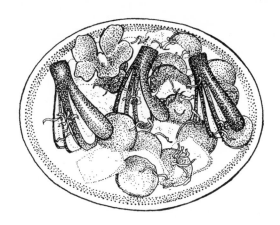

Bobotie

Cooked and flaked hake, cod, or haddock can be substituted for beef.

30 ml/2 tbs vegetable oil
2 large onions
Two 15-ml spoons/2 tbs mild
  curry powder
1 heaped 15-ml spoon/1 heaped tbs
  granulated sugar
30–45 ml/2–3 tbs meat stock or
  water
1¼ kg/2½ lb best minced or ground
  beef (lamb or pork can
  substitute)
1 large egg, beaten
1 slice white bread, soaked in milk,
  mashed, and squeezed
3 cloves garlic, peeled and crushed
  with salt

15 blanched, slivered almonds
5 or 6 dried and thinly-sliced
  apricots or pears
1 heaped 15-ml spoon/1 heaped tbs
  apricot jam
Two 5-ml spoons/2 teasp chopped
  fennel leaves
One 5-ml spoon/1 teasp ground
  turmeric
One 15-ml spoon/1 tbs pumpkin
  seeds, if available
15 ml/1 tbs virgin marsala or
  medium sherry
Lemon juice, salt, and pepper to
  taste

Topping
6 fresh lemon leaves, or vine
  leaves in brine
3 large eggs

360 ml/12 fl oz/1½ cups milk
Salt and pepper

Heat the oil in a very large sauté pan while peeling and finely chopping the onions. Sauté these until soft and golden, add curry powder and sugar and cook, stirring occasionally, for about 2 minutes. Add meat stock and minced beef, well-crumbled, and all remaining ingredients except those for the topping. Simmer, stirring, for 5 minutes. Check seasoning, which should be interesting but not overpowering.

Butter a large oval baking dish of about 38 × 30 × 6½ cm/15 × 12 × 2½ in deep – or two smaller ones – and pour in the *bobotie* mixture. The dish(es) can then be well-wrapped and frozen, if you choose. Thaw before proceeding to the next step, which is to soften the lemon or vine leaves by parboiling them for several minutes; dry well, and cover the meat with these.

Beat together the eggs and milk, season, and pour this savoury custard over all. Bake in a 180°C/350°F/gas mark 4 oven for 40–45 minutes, or until set. Serve hot in the baking dish.

Yellow rice with raisins

480 g/16 oz long-grain rice,
   well-washed
Two 5-ml spoons/2 teasp each salt
   and ground turmeric
1½ × 15-ml spoons/1½ tbs light
   brown or granulated sugar

30 g/1 oz butter
1 stick cinnamon
180 g/6 oz raisins
Pepper

Bring 1 litre/35 fl oz/4½ cups of water to the boil, stir in salt and all other ingredients except the raisins and pepper, bring back to the boil, cover, and simmer the rice gently until it has absorbed most of the liquid (about 15 minutes). Add raisins and stir gently, replace lid and continue to cook the rice over a low heat until it is tender and has completely absorbed the water (about 5 minutes more). Remove cinnamon, add pepper, check seasoning, and serve the rice on a hot platter.

Both recipes from Betty Long, Surrey Hills branch, England

Sambals
as described on page 163, plus

Plum chutney
This makes roughly 2½–2¾ kg/5–6 lbs.

240 g/8 oz each raisins and
   sultanas (yellow raisins)
1900 g/4 lb plums
180 g/6 oz each onions and
   shallots
1 large clove garlic
Two 5-ml spoons/2 teasp cayenne
   pepper

One 15-ml spoon/1 tbs each salt
   and ground ginger
960 g/2 lb/generous 5 cups brown
   sugar
300 ml/½ pint/1¼ cups white wine
   vinegar

Chop the raisins and sultanas, stone and chop the plums, finely chop the peeled onions, shallots, and garlic. Put all into a preserving pan or large, heavy saucepan with the seasonings, sugar and vinegar. Simmer uncovered, stirring frequently, until the fruit is cooked and the mixture has reached a thick consistency but is still a little runny (30–45 minutes). Pour the chutney into hot, sterilised glass jars and seal them at once.

George Rainbird, Gloucestershire, England,
and former Society Chairman

A pair of black bottom pies

Ample helpings for everyone.

Crusts
135 g/4½ oz butter, unsalted if possible
360 g/12 oz ginger biscuits or ginger snaps

A little dessicated coconut, unsweetened
Icing (confectioners') sugar, if needed

Mousse
420 g/14 oz semi-sweet chocolate
210 g/7 oz butter, unsalted if possible
5 g/1 teasp powdered gelatine or 1 leaf European gelatine

Dark rum
6 eggs
Two 15-ml spoons/2 tbs icing (confectioners') sugar

Topping
180 ml/6 fl oz/¾ cup thick cream
Castor (granulated) sugar to taste
15 ml/1 tbs lemon juice

Grated lemon zest
Grated semi-sweet chocolate

To make the crusts, melt and cool the butter, crush the ginger biscuits and combine both with a little coconut and – if necessary – sugar to taste. Butter two shallow 23 cm/9 in metal pie plates whose sides don't slope excessively, divide the ginger mixture in two and press each half firmly over the bottom and up the sides of each pie dish. Crusts should be thick and crumbly. Bake them at 165°C/325°F/gas mark 3 for about 15 minutes, and cool.

Prepare the mousse by melting broken chocolate with butter in a heavy saucepan which you have set, covered, into a large pan of just-boiled water. Reheat water as necessary to melt the chocolate.

Soften the gelatine in cool water; melt it, swirling, in a minimum of water over a low heat. When the chocolate and butter are ready, beat them smooth, remove the saucepan from its larger pan and stir the mixture to cool it slightly. Strain in the gelatine, add a healthy dash of rum, separate the eggs and beat in the yolks.

Whip the egg whites to soft peaks, whisk in icing or confectioners' sugar until peaks are firm, and beat $\frac{1}{4}$ of the whites into the chocolate base to lighten it. Pour chocolate onto the remaining whites and fold all together deftly. Divide the mousse between the two crusts and chill them for several hours.

Remove the pies from the refrigerator about $1–1\frac{1}{2}$ hours before serving and cover each with a thin layer of slightly sweetened whipped cream into which lemon juice and a little grated zest have been stirred at the end of whisking. Shave chocolate over the centre of both pies and bring them, eventually, to the buffet.

Autumn fruit salad

900 ml/1½ pints/1 quart fruity
   white wine
90 ml/6 tbs honey
1400 g/3 lb mixed autumn fruits
   such as fresh figs, white and
   black grapes, plums, plus others,
like melon and kiwi, which may
   be obtainable without vast
   expense
2 pomegranates, if available
Lemon juice to taste

Simmer the wine and honey together for 10 minutes to vaporise alcohol and mellow the flavours. Quarter figs and halve grapes, seeding grapes if necessary, but peel neither. Peel plums after immersing them in just-boiled water (reserve peelings), quarter and stone them. Make melon balls and peel and slice kiwi or whatever else you choose. Add all their juices to the sweetened wine and poach each fruit separately and gently until it is just cooked. If melon and kiwi are quite ripe don't poach, but put them directly into a serving bowl. With a slotted spoon, remove each poached fruit in turn from wine to bowl. When all have been dealt with, add plum and any other edible peelings to the liquid and boil it down to a syrupy consistency. Let it cool, and strain the syrup over the fruit. Halve one pomegranate and squeeze it like an orange, strain and mix the juice into the salad, taste, and judge whether to add the juice of the second pomegranate. Add lemon juice to suit, mix well, and serve the salad chilled.

A tasting of terrines
for six to eight

MUSHROOMS AND LEEKS IN A SPINACH PARCEL,
GREEN VINAIGRETTE

TERRINE OF TROUT, WATERCRESS MAYONNAISE

SMOKED MACKEREL PÂTÉ

NUT-STUDDED PÂTÉ OF CHICKEN LIVERS

PHEASANT TERRINE, ONION PRESERVE

BREADS, BISCUITS, ASSORTED RAW VEGETABLES

A PAIR OF CHEDDAR APPLE TARTS

A tasting of terrines
for six to eight

An agreeable way to entertain friends who know each other well and are interested in the nuances of good cooking is to take a theme and ring its changes. In the case of terrines, called after the earthenware vessels in which many are baked, you have a spectrum of possibilities from the amazing vegetable pyramids bound by the slightest whisp of aspic – and of course *not* baked – to elaborate game layers marinated and truffled and sealed in pastry. The latter are the real pâtés, or pies, named for their wrapping – but colloquially, cooks sweep puréed chicken livers, potted fish, and other rustic concoctions into that rather loose appellation.

As it happens, we were sent four variations on this theme, and adding a fifth, realised that we had a tasting ready-made and on the table. Our own terrine is the mushroom and leeks, which is somewhat like a six-sided quiche wrapped up in spinach with a spinach vinaigrette to sharpen it. This leads to Gail Wright's delicate layers of trout fillets bound with trout mousse and coloured with watercress, and on to Kitty Wiersum's much more robust smoked mackerel pâté that's flavoured with horseradish and should definitely swagger.

Raymond Norlin sent us chicken livers, but poached in a clove-scented broth as a change from the orthodox tossing in butter, and we put toasted macadamias and pistachios with the smooth liver for an added texture. As number five, Maurice Kidd's pheasant terrine, optionally truffled – a classic recipe and always delicious. Serve it with a variation of Michel Guérard's sweet-sour *confiture d'oignons*.

A tasting like this should be unreeled as a buffet, with a selection of breads – some of them toasted – and what the British call "biscuits" and the Americans "crackers", good butter and an assortment of quickly prepared *crudités* like carrots, celery, radishes, leaves of Belgian endive or chicory, or whatever you like that is available. There'll be plenty to eat, and the five terrines are obviously not to be piled willy-nilly onto plates, but tasted one at a time with comparative forays between.

Then, at the end, everything is swept away and replaced by two buttery, lemony, and very homespun apple pies, tart enough to bring out the cheese in their pastry – the same cheesy shortcrust as for the cocktail party turnovers, but used here to quite a different effect.

The best season for this tasting would be autumn, not just due to the copious food, but because autumn is the time for excellent apples and never-frozen pheasant. No matter what people say, thawed game is not as good for any purpose as the recently-killed and well-hung animal.

The plan of battle is to make the pheasant terrine at least five days before serving, then the liver and mackerel, the terrine of trout, and one day ahead, the spinach parcel. Prepare condiments and tarts on the morning or afternoon of the tasting.

AWS

There used to be a wine advertising campaign which featured an awkward fellow named Rosco. His particular foible when dining in a restaurant was always to order something different from everyone else. If the party wanted beef, Rosco chose lobster mayonnaise; if others craved grilled sole, Rosco demanded roast plover. The advertiser's answer to the host's dilemma about wine was of course his own brand, which had the virtue – apparently – of "going with anything". We suspect that one day an exasperated host ordered Rosco a carafe of cyanide, since he has now vanished from our daily papers.

Rosco's creator would be in his element here, for what indeed complements meat and game, smoked fish and fresh, chicken livers and cheese-with-apples? One solution might be water, another the light, not-too-dry white wines of Southern England, which unkind Frenchmen have been known to say taste anyway of *eau minérale*. Their own rosés of Marsannay and Sancerre, or the ubiquitous rieslings, would all be appreciated.

Many people are happy to drink beaujolais, or another good gamay, with fish or meat, and lovers of the cheerfully sparkling red lambrusco – described by a Tuscan winemaker as "Italy's answer to Pepsi-Cola" – will have no problems. The great American authority on Italian wines, Burton Anderson, notes that Frank Schoonmaker's *Encyclopedia* called this "as nearly undrinkable as a well-known wine could be". In the latest edition, Julius Wile omits this slander and remarks that lambrusco accounts for more than half the Italian wine drunk in the USA.

You may detect a pattern in the cornucopia of tastes that we've proposed. There are no citrus fruits, chocolate, coffee, malt vinegar, excessive picklings or curry – all enemies of wine. Nor is there too much garlic or cream or sugar. So we suggest you bring on several of the bottles we mention – including the water, mineral of course – and just let 'em loose!

HD-M

Mushrooms and leeks in a spinach parcel

270–300 g/9–10 oz fresh or frozen
  – but thawed – spinach, weighed
  after stalking, cooking (if fresh),
  and squeezing thoroughly of
  water
75 g/2½ oz butter
120 g/4 oz leeks, weighed after
  washing and trimming

3 shallots
3 large cloves garlic
720 g/1½ lb button mushrooms
Salt
6 eggs
2 egg whites
Pepper

Lightly butter a 1½ litre/2½ pint/1½ quart oblong terrine or loaf tin. Melt 15 g/½ oz of butter in a sauté pan and heat the spinach through, stirring to dry it further and to prevent burning. Season, and with the aid of a fork, line the terrine, starting with the bottom and working up each side, with a thin and cohesive layer of spinach.

Melt the remaining butter in 2 large sauté pans, slice the leeks, peel and thinly slice the shallots, peel and mince the garlic. Divide these between the pans and sauté over a low heat for about 3 minutes. Thinly slice the mushrooms, wash and drain them thoroughly, add half to each pan, salt and cook them uncovered on a medium heat until the copious liquid expelled has evaporated and the mixture is dry. Remove from the heat and transfer all to a large heavy saucepan.

Thoroughly beat the eggs and whites and add them to the saucepan. Season well to taste. With a wooden spoon stir continuously over a low heat until the mixture starts to thicken like a smooth sauce and the eggs become slightly opaque but don't begin to scramble. Pour this immediately into the prepared terrine and place it uncovered in a *bain-marie* of hot water to come half-way up the sides. Transfer this to a 155°C/310°F/gas mark 2 oven and bake it for about an hour, or until a skewer plunged into the middle tests fairly hot on the back of your hand.

Cool the terrine, slice away any ragged edges of spinach, and refrigerate, covered. To turn it out the next day, you may need to dip the container briefly into hot water and run the blunt edge of a knife carefully round the inside.

Serve at room temperature, slicing through the green "wrapping" to the mushroom-flecked interior, and accompany the slices with the following sauce.

Green vinaigrette

300 g/10 oz stalked, cooked, and
   well-dried spinach
2 or 3 shallots
75 ml/5 tbs vinaigrette made from

wine vinegar, mustard, olive oil,
   and seasonings, garlic omitted
   (page 221)
Salt and pepper

Coarsely chop the spinach, peel and mince the shallots, using 3 of them if small, combine with vinaigrette and season well. Serve at room temperature.

Terrine of trout, watercress mayonnaise

6–8 fresh trout, enough to yield
   960 g/2 lb flesh after boning
1 shallot
A few coriander seeds
A few black peppercorns
300 ml/½ pint/1¼ cups dry white
   wine
2 oz watercress leaves

Salt
1 egg
1 egg yolk
150 ml/5 fl oz/scant ⅔ cup cream
Cayenne pepper
Pepper
Mayonnaise flavoured with lemon
   and watercress

Fillet and skin the fish, removing all small bones. Reserve half the fillets, halve them across, and cut them lengthwise into strips.

Peel and mince the shallot, bruise the coriander and peppercorns, add these to the white wine and boil all together for 5 minutes to infuse the flavours. Cool. Throw the watercress leaves into boiling salted water, bring water back to a good brief boil, drain and refresh the cress immediately. Squeeze away its residual water and chop finely.

Stiffen the strips of trout by bringing them slowly _just_ to the boil in the infused wine. Remove wine from the heat and the fish from the wine, cool and dry the fillets. Strain the wine and reduce a few ounces of it to about 30 ml/2 tbs. Pour this over the fillets, and use the remainder for stock elsewhere.

Put the uncooked trout, plus the egg and yolk, into a food processor, steel blade in place, and purée until very, very smooth. Transfer the fish to a bowl set into a larger bowl lined with ice, and gradually beat in the cream. Season well with salt, pepper, and a pinch of cayenne, but don't beat excessively after seasoning or the purée could separate. Remove $\frac{2}{3}$ of this mousse and mix the watercress into the remainder.

Butter a $1\frac{1}{4}$ litre/2 pint/5 cup terrine and cover the bottom with half the rosy purée. Lay half the fillets in rows along the top, grind on salt and pepper, cover with all the green purée, then the remaining fillets, well-seasoned, and finally the rosy mousse.

Rap the terrine smartly on the work surface, wet your hand and repeatedly smooth the top of the mousse. Cover the terrine with two layers of buttered foil and refrigerate for at least an hour.

Bake the mousse in a *bain-marie* as in "spinach parcel" above, in a 180°C/350°F/gas mark 4 oven, turning once, for about an hour, or until a skewer plunged into the middle tests quite hot.

Cool the terrine, uncovered, to room temperature, tip it gently to drain thoroughly of liquid, cover with plastic wrap and refrigerate overnight.

Serve, about an hour out of the refrigerator, in the cleaned container, removing slices carefully. Accompany them with a good lemony home-made mayonnaise into which you've stirred, at the last minute, some finely-chopped leaves of watercress.

Gail Wright, South Bank branch, London, England

Smoked mackerel pâté

2 smoked mackerel weighing about
   240 g/8 oz each, or similar
   smoked fish of equivalent weight
   if mackerel are unobtainable
60 g/2 oz butter, melted and
   cooled
60 ml/4 tbs dry white wine

45 ml/3 tbs lemon juice
$1\frac{1}{2}$ × 5-ml spoons/$1\frac{1}{2}$ teasp grated
   horseradish
One 2.5-ml spoon/$\frac{1}{2}$ teasp paprika
Salt and pepper
60 ml/4 tbs sour cream

Remove the skin and all bones from the mackerel and put the flesh, which will total about 360 g/12 oz, into the bowl of a food processor.

Add butter, wine, lemon juice, horseradish, paprika, salt, and pepper and purée until all the ingredients are combined but not overly smooth. Whiz in the sour cream, taste, add more of the four seasonings if required. The result should be well-flavoured.

Beat the purée thoroughly, and pile it into an attractive terrine or serving dish. Level and striate the top, cover it tightly with plastic wrap and refrigerate for at least two days; it improves significantly if kept firmly covered.

Remove the terrine to room temperature about half an hour before serving, and scoop it by the spoonful to eat with toast.

Kitty Wiersum, Surrey, England

Nut-studded pâté of chicken livers

60 g/2 oz macadamia nuts, or blanched almonds if these are unavailable
60 g/2 oz shelled pistachios
Two 5-ml spoons/2 teasp each black peppercorns and whole cloves
3 bay leaves
A few parsley stalks
1¼ kg/2½ lb fresh chicken livers
1 small onion
2 large cloves garlic

Two 5-ml spoons/2 teasp dry mustard
Big pinch of grated nutmeg
Tabasco sauce
One 5-ml spoon/1 teasp or more of salt
Pepper
About 30 ml/2 tbs brandy
240 g/8 oz lightly-salted butter, soft but not runny
240 g/8 oz butter, clarified

Slice macadamias or almonds into thirds, skin pistachios by blanching them for a minute in boiling water, draining, and rubbing away their skins in a towel. Toast the nuts together in a 180°C/350°F/gas mark 4 oven for 5–10 minutes or until they begin to colour. Cool.

Fill a very large saucepan with 2 litres/3 pints/2 quarts water, add peppercorns, cloves, bay leaves, and parsley, bring water to the boil, simmer 10 minutes, strain and reserve. Clean the livers, cut away connective tissue and any green stains, and poach them in this broth, at a bare simmer, for about 10 minutes or until just cooked and still slightly pink inside. Drain the livers and transfer them to a blender or food processor. Reserve the broth.

Peel and mince onion and garlic, add them, with mustard, nutmeg, dashes of tabasco sauce, one 5-ml spoon/1 teasp of salt, pepper, and the brandy to livers and blend till smooth. Cool, add the first amount of butter and 30–45 ml/2–3 tbs of the cooking liquid. Blend again till smooth as silk but not runny. Check for seasoning, remembering that chilling deadens flavour and salt. Use the remaining poaching liquid as a basis for soup.

Remove the pâté to a bowl, fold in the toasted nuts, and pile the mixture into a 2 litre/3 pint/2 quart terrine. Smooth the top and cover tightly with plastic wrap, refrigerate, and when the pâté has set, seal it with clarified butter made as follows.

Melt the remaining 240 g/8 oz butter in a saucepan, allow it to stand, skim away the froth, then spoon the clear yellow liquid away from the milky solids. Put the latter aside and run the clear butter over the set pâté. Refrigerate, uncovered, until the butter has hardened, then wrap the terrine in foil. Allow to mellow for at least 3 days. If uncut, it can live on, refrigerated, for a couple of weeks.

Serve the pâté in its terrine, and scoop or cut out successive helpings.

Raymond H. Norlin, Northern Illinois Wine & Food Society, USA

Pheasant terrine

This can also be made with two guinea fowl, or with one guinea fowl and one pigeon, if the latter is not too old and tough.

1 young cock pheasant of about 960 g/2 lb prepared weight	240 g/8 oz each lean veal and rindless sliced streaky (belly)
90 ml/3 fl oz/generous ⅓ cup brandy	bacon, unsmoked
A large pinch each of dried thyme, marjoram, and chives	1 egg
	Ground mace or grated nutmeg
2 bay leaves	8 juniper berries
Chopped truffles (optional)	1–2 × 5-ml spoons/1–2 teasp salt
360 g/12 oz fresh belly of pork, weighed without rind	Pepper
	Lard to seal

Roast the pheasant for 10 minutes at 205°C/400°F/gas mark 6, and cool it; this makes the bird easier to skin and bone.

Skin the carcass and cut the breast into enough long, thin strips to make up two layers in an oblong terrine of 1400 ml/2¼ pints/5½ cups capacity; put these to marinate with the brandy, three dried herbs, bay leaves, and truffles if used, turning the mixture several times.

Cut the remaining pheasant from its bones, denerve it, denerve the pork belly and veal and cut away their connective tissue, take up half the bacon, and cut all of these – plus any extra breast meat – into cubes. Either put the cubes through the coarse disk of a meat grinder, or chop them well by hand, or run them round the food processor until the consistency is that of coarsely-chopped. Pick out any nervous tissue that may have eluded you.

Meanwhile, make a good stock from the pheasant skin and picked-over carcass by simmering them in lightly-salted water for several hours. Sieve the stock and reduce it to the value of 120 ml/4 fl oz/½ cup.

Put the mixed meats into a bowl, add the beaten egg, some mace or nutmeg, crushed juniper berries, one 5-ml spoon/1 tsp salt, and plenty of pepper. Pour in a little of the breasts' marinade plus all the cooled, reduced stock. Mix this forcemeat well, cover and refrigerate overnight, along with the covered, marinating breast meat.

The next day, line a terrine of the above-mentioned dimensions with the remaining bacon (saving a little to cover the top), pour the breasts' marinade, minus bay leaves, into the forcemeat, mix well, and fry a little ball of this to test for seasoning. Add salt and so forth if necessary; the terrine should be quite savoury.

Press a third of the forcemeat along the terrine's base, lay half the strips of breast meat in rows along the top, grind on salt and pepper, cover with half the remaining forcemeat, another layer of seasoned breast, and the final amount of forcemeat. Rap terrine on the work surface, round and smooth the top, press on the remaining bacon.

Cover the terrine with a double layer of foil and the lid, bake in a *bain-marie* at 165°C/325°F/gas mark 3, turning once, for about 1½–2 hours or till the terrine tests hot in the centre. Remove lid and foil for the final 15 minutes to colour the top.

Place the terrine on a plate, replace the foil and cover the top with a board or brick that just fits inside the rim. Weight the board with heavy cans or scale weights, and when the filling is cool, refrigerate, still weighted, overnight.

Next day, remove the bacon wrapping, clean the container with a sponge and some salt, melt about 180 g/6 oz pure lard and pour it on in a thick layer to seal the forcemeat from all contact with air. Chill and mature the terrine, refrigerated, for 4–5 days at least. (Uncut, it will keep for two weeks). Serve sliced, with small spoonfuls of the garnish which follows.

Maurice Kidd, East Lothian, Scotland

Onion preserve

We like Michel Guérard's idea of offering game terrines with a sort of onion relish, what the French call a *marmelade*, but find his recipe a bit too sweet and buttery. So we've adapted it and introduced a little marmalade in the *British* sense – made from bitter oranges – that gives an unexpected dimension.

Large onions weighing a total of about 1 kg/2¼ lb unpeeled	Two 15-ml spoons/2 tbs coarse-cut, dark, and bitter orange marmalade
90 g/3 oz butter	
Salt	120 ml/4 fl oz/½ cup red wine vinegar
Two 15-ml spoons/2 tbs granulated sugar	Pepper
60 ml/4 tbs brandy	

Peel the onions and slice them very, very thin. Melt the butter in a large heavy saucepan – or two of medium size – add the onions and a pinch of salt, cover the pan and sweat the contents over a very low heat, stirring periodically, until they soften, which takes 30–40 minutes. Stir in the sugar and continue to cook and slowly caramelise the onions, covered, for half an hour more.

Add brandy, marmalade, and vinegar, stir, and go on cooking the now-uncovered onions on the same heat for 45 minutes or so further, stirring often, until the mixture, well-condensed, has turned a lovely russet-brown. Season to taste, pour off any excess butter, cool and refrigerate. If you like, this can be made days ahead without harm to anyone.

Serve this preserve just barely heated through to revive its gloss and pliancy.

A pair of Cheddar apple tarts

If Cheddar is out of the question, use an appropriate substitute.

One recipe Cheddar cheese pastry, page 152	6 or 7 large, tart, and firm cooking apples

60 g/2 oz/⅓ cup light brown sugar
Two 15-ml spoons/2 tbs cornflour
  (cornstarch)
A heaped 1.25-ml spoon/1 heaped
  ¼ teasp, or more, ground
  cinnamon

A big pinch of grated nutmeg
90 g/3 oz butter, unsalted if
  possible
45 ml/3 tbs lemon juice

Make and chill the pastry, bring it to room temperature, roll out ⅔ of it and line two 20 cm/8 in flan rings set onto heavy baking sheets. Refrigerate to firm the pastry.

Peel, core, and slice the apples thinly, sieve sugar with cornflour (cornstarch) and spices and toss with the apples. Judge whether more spices are needed; they should not be too evident. Pile the apples into each pastry, alternating with flakes of butter and drops of lemon juice, being liberal with butter and lemon over the tops.

Roll out the remaining pastry and cover both tarts with a lattice crust, binding the edge of each with a neat strip of dough.

Bake tarts for 10 minutes at 220°C/425°F/gas mark 7, then lower the oven to 190°C/375°F/gas mark 5 and bake for a further 25–30 minutes or until pastry is golden-brown and the apples' syrup is bubbling.

Cool the tarts on a rack, and, if making them early in the day, reheat sufficiently to serve warm.

Additions

As our twenty menus evolved, so did a pile of recipes which we couldn't bear to leave out! So we've brought them in as delicious additions, and sometimes alternatives, ranging from Burmese chicken to Grandfather's egg – the latter, possibly, our secret single favourite in the entire book.

Following these are recurring basics which we've assembled at the end for easy reference: three broths, a vinaigrette, three pastries. And then, a send-off for all good menus.

For the first course

Brain cakes

An old family recipe of Anne Kidd's; we find it delectable, and suggest a little warmed tomato sauce as accompaniment. Serves 4.

Brains from 4 lambs' heads
Salt
1 each carrot, onion, and bay leaf
6 peppercorns
30 ml/2 tbs lemon juice
One–two 15-ml spoons/1–2 tbs
  finely-chopped parsley

60 g/2 oz fresh breadcrumbs
1–2 eggs
Pepper
30 g/1 oz butter
Tomato sauce

Soak brains in lightly-salted water overnight, then peel away their outer membranes – a process which can be fiddly and difficult; if you really can't manage it, don't worry. Rinse the brains well of any blood.

Make a poaching liquid with the peeled, sliced carrot and onion, plus bay leaf and a little salt and ample water; bring all to the boil and simmer for 15 minutes. Turn the heat down, add peppercorns and lemon juice, slip brains into the broth and simmer them, half-covered, for 15 minutes more.

Remove brains from the liquid (which can be strained and used as a soup base), cool and finely chop them. Add parsley to taste, about 20 g/ ¾ oz breadcrumbs and enough beaten egg to bind without making the brains too moist. Season well with salt and pepper and stir over a very

184

low heat for about 5 minutes until the mixture thickens. Cool, and form into 8 oval cakes.

Roll the cakes in beaten egg, cover them with breadcrumbs and shake off the excess. Sauté in butter over a gentle heat until golden and browning.

Serve hot, 2 per person, with a spoonful each of heated tomato sauce.

Anne Kidd, East Lothian, Scotland

Snails in the Alsatian manner

Snails without garlic, and tasting very *green*. They originated with Adolphe Willm of Barr in the French province of Alsace, shippers of local wines and formerly of snails. Instead of snail dishes for baking, we prefer Jane Grigson's method of heating the shells on slices of bread, which absorb the sauce and are eaten along with the gastropods. Makes 2½ dozen.

30 g/1 oz peeled shallots
15 g/½ oz very fresh parsley without stalks
240 g/8 oz softened butter
120 ml/4 fl oz/½ cup riesling or sylvaner or similar dry but light and fruity white wine

Pepper
2½ dozen canned snails and their shells
Large slices of whole meal or whole wheat bread, cut 1½ cm/½ in thick, plus more bread for mopping up sauce

Slice the shallots and roughly chop the parsley, put with the butter into the bowl of a blender or food processor, begin to blend, and slowly pour the wine through the top opening, blending until a smooth paste forms. Grind in pepper and re-blend.

Drain snails – which have been cooked during the canning process and can be quite salty – into a colander. Wash and drain the shells, fill each with a little of the butter, a snail, then butter up to the shell's rim.

Cut holes in the sliced bread with an apple corer, put bread onto heavy, buttered baking sheets, and balance a shell in each hole. Heat at 205°C/400°F/gas mark 6 for 15–20 minutes until the sauce begins to bubble. The bread toasts and becomes the perfect, crunchy vehicle for overflowing butter.

Serve shells on their toasts, and pass extra bread for disposing of sauce.

Julius Wile, New York Wine & Food Society, USA

Apple-raisin soup

Both tart and sweet, with an interesting texture. Serves 4.

720 g/1½ lb tart cooking apples, unpeeled
900 ml/1½ pints/1 quart dry red wine
2 slices white bread
3 thick slices lemon
One 5 cm/2 in stick cinnamon
3 whole cloves with heads removed

Pinch of salt
30 g/1 oz butter
45 g/1½ oz granulated sugar
90 g/3 oz sultanas (yellow raisins)
1 egg yolk
10 ml/2 teasp brandy
Sour cream and powdered cinnamon for garnish

Wash, slice, and core the apples and place them, with the wine, bread, lemon, spices, and salt in a saucepan to simmer until the apples are tender. Remove lemon, cinnamon stick, and cloves, squeeze lemon juice back into the mixture, cool it slightly and purée in a blender or food processor. The soup can be made in advance to this point and refrigerated.

To finish, heat the mixture with the butter, sugar, and sultanas or yellow raisins, bring to the boil – stirring to prevent sticking – and simmer for 5 minutes. Whisk brandy into the egg yolk, whisk in a little of the hot liquid to warm the yolk, and beat this into the soup. Stir briefly over a low heat – not allowing the soup to boil, which would curdle the egg – and serve in four heated bowls, garnished with a fillip of sour cream and a dusting of cinnamon.

Joan and Robert Hamilton, Honolulu Wine & Food Society, USA

Lakeside smokies

Conceived for the Scotch hot-smoked haddock known as Arbroath or Aberdeen smokies, these can also be made with smoked mackerel or herring. We found that frozen fish works well. Serves 8 as a filling first course, or 4 – allowing 2 ramekins per person – as the core of an informal late supper. Clive de Paula recommends manzanilla or a pale cortado sherry as escorts.

240 ml/8 fl oz/1 cup thick cream
Two 240 g/8 oz Arbroath or
    Aberdeen smokies, or like weight
    of other smoked fish
Pepper

4 tomatoes of 90–120 g/3–4 oz
    each
Two 15-ml spoons/2 tbs
    finely-chopped onion
Grated Parmesan cheese

Lightly butter eight ramekin dishes of 150 ml/5 fl oz/scant ⅔ cup capacity, and put 15 ml/1 tbs cream into each.

Skin, fillet, and flake the fish, being careful to remove all bones, and divide it among the ramekins. Grind on pepper.

Peel, seed, and chop the tomatoes, drain away any excess moisture, combine with onion, and spread this over the fish. Add pepper – salt is unlikely to be necessary – top each ramekin with a further 15 ml/1 tbs cream, and sprinkle on some cheese. At this point, the smokies can be loosely covered and refrigerated until needed.

When ready, bake them at 180°C/350°F/gas mark 4 for 30 minutes. Serve brown and bubbling.

F. Clive de Paula, London branch, England and former Society
Chairman

Caviar and new potatoes Stanford Court

Baked potatoes with sour cream is a long-time American favourite which Fournou's Ovens, the restaurant of the Stanford Court Hotel in San Francisco, has turned into a splendid vehicle for the recently-revived American caviar: the golden roe of Great Lakes' whitefish, the black eggs from Northwestern and New England sturgeon. If you are not in America, you'll have to make do with the Russian substitute! But *don't* use lumpfish. Serves 6.

James Nassikas is President of the Stanford Court Hotel and was an early '70s pioneer in stocking its cellars with an excellent variety of California wines.

12 small, waxy new potatoes
480–600 g/1–1¼ lb rock salt
Oil

About 120 ml/4 fl oz/½ cup sour
   cream
About eight 15-ml spoons/8 tbs
   golden or black caviar

Scrub and dry the potatoes, leaving skins intact. Spread the rock salt over a large baking dish and cover with potatoes – salt will draw out their moisture and make them flakier. Bake for 30–35 minutes in a 230°C/450°F/gas mark 8 oven until tender. Keep the salt hot and remove the potatoes.

Slice potatoes in half the long way, carefully scoop out all their pulp, mash, and keep it warm.

Heat enough oil for deep-frying to 190°C/375°F, drop in the potato shells a few at a time and fry them quickly until crisp and golden-brown. Drain well on absorbent paper.

Fill the shells with the mashed potato. Top each with a spoonful or so of sour cream and about one 5-ml spoon/1 teasp of caviar. Serve on a bed of the hot rock salt, and give 2 potatoes – 4 halves – to each person.

James A. Nassikas, San Francisco and Marin County Wine & Food
Societies, California, USA

Œufs mollets en meurette

A variation of the classic Burgundian dish usually made by poaching the eggs in wine. It made Madame de Sévigné tipsy enough to feel bound to offer a special confession. Serves 6.

750 ml/1¼ pints/3 cups red
  burgundy or similar wine of the
  pinot noir or gamay grape
45 g/1½ oz each diced onion and
  carrot
1 bay leaf
A sprig each of parsley and thyme
1 large clove garlic
Salt

75 g/2½ oz each whole button
  mushrooms and slices of rindless
  bacon cut ½–¾ cm/³⁄₁₆ in thick
Butter if needed
Pepper
30 g/1 oz each flour and softened
  butter
6 eggs
6 triangles of toast

Pour the wine into a saucepan and add onion, carrot, herbs, crushed garlic, and a scant pinch of salt. Simmer until the wine is reduced to half its volume.

Meanwhile, thinly slice and wash the mushrooms, cut the bacon into small lardons. Briefly fry the lardons in a small pan until crisp, remove them and toss the mushrooms over a high heat in the rendered fat – supplemented by butter if need be – until cooked. Drain.

Strain the wine, return it to the saucepan, add bacon and mushrooms, pepper, and more salt if necessary. Make a *beurre manié* by working the flour and butter into a paste.

Bring a large pan of water to the boil and lower into it 6 eggs. Let them boil slowly for exactly 5 minutes. Remove them, cool under cold water, crack and carefully peel away the shells. The whites will be set and the yolks soft.

Warm eggs in a bowl of hot water while toasting 6 triangles of bread and reheating the wine and its additives to the simmer. Off the heat, whisk in the *beurre manié*, return pan to the flame, and simmer the wine for 1 minute, stirring. The thickened result should just coat the back of a spoon. Check seasoning, put toast into six soup plates, top each with a well-drained egg, pour on the sauce, and serve.

Sandy Bibby, Hiraethog Wine & Food Society, Wales

Saffron squid

A sort of rich soup that serves 4.

2 squid, fresh or frozen, totalling
  about 900 g/just under 2 lb
  untrimmed

1 litre/35 fl oz/4½ cups broth made
  with squids' tentacles
Salt

4 large cloves garlic   120 g/4 oz butter
A handful of fresh basil leaves   Pepper
A pinch of saffron threads or a   4 oz rice ·
  1.25-ml spoon/¼ teasp powdered
  saffron

Prepare the squid as for squid Chinese-style on page 126, reserving the pouches and fins. Make the fish broth by boiling the tentacles in lightly-salted water for 15 minutes. Peel and mince the garlic, shred the basil – reserving some of the leaves for decoration – add the garlic and shredded basil with saffron, butter, and a little salt to the unstrained broth and boil 15 minutes longer.

Slice the squid pouches and fins into small strips, strain the broth, and poach the squid for about an hour, until tender.

Towards the end of this time, pour in more water to adjust the amount and flavour of the liquid, add the rice, well-washed, and when this has cooked, adjust seasoning and serve the squid in soup bowls with basil leaves as ornament.

J. A. Witter, New South Wales Wine & Food Society, Australia

Fish, meat, poultry, and game

Fillets of sole with almonds

"Black" sole means the so-called Dover sole, and this recipe is a variation of *sole meunière*. At a pinch, substitute very fresh fillets of whiting or American flounder. Serves 2–3.

6 fillets of black sole, or
    appropriate substitute
A small quantity of flour, seasoned
    with salt and pepper
120 g/4 oz butter

90 g/3 oz blanched and split
    almonds
5 ml/1 teasp lemon juice
More salt and pepper

Wash the fillets if necessary, pat them dry, and coat them with the seasoned flour, shaking away the excess.

In order not to burn the butter in which you sauté the fish, clarify 90 g/3 oz of it by melting and letting it rest, scooping off the foam, and pouring the golden liquid carefully away from its white solids.

Heat this liquid to foaming in a large frying pan – or two smaller ones – lay in the fillets and sauté them over a moderate heat until golden-brown. Turn carefully and lightly brown the other side. Drain the fish, keep it hot on a serving plate, wipe the frying pan – or one of them if using two – and reheat it with the remaining 30 g/1 oz butter. Drop in the almonds and toss them over a medium heat until they too turn golden and browning. Add lemon juice and toss again.

191

Pour this quickly over the fish, grind on salt and pepper and serve immediately.

Olive Cusack, Limerick Wine & Food Society, Ireland

Barbecue salmon

We haven't tried this; perhaps it's delicious! The contributor has swapped its recipe for the secrets of Louis Outhier's three-starred turbot in champagne sauce from l'Oasis restaurant, at la Napoule in the South of France. Serves 6–8.

One 2–2¾ kg/4–6 lb salmon
1 bottle Canadian, American, or
   Australian beer, or European
   lager – or equivalent

240 ml/8 fl oz/1 cup dark soy
   sauce
180 g/6 oz/1 cup brown sugar
Garlic mayonnaise

Fillet the salmon, skin on, and cut it into serving pieces. Mix together the beer, soy sauce, and sugar and marinate the fish in this overnight in the refrigerator, or for at least 6 hours at room temperature, basting occasionally.

Grill the pieces skin side down above a deep bed of coals without flames for 14 minutes on one side, basting with the marinade. Lift the salmon carefully off its burned skin, which will adhere to the barbecue rack, and turn the fish over. Grill it, basting, for another 12 minutes.

Serve warm or cold with a garlic mayonnaise.

Dr. Stanley Oleksiuk, Windsor, Ontario Wine & Food Society, Canada

Striped bass in phyllo pastry, beurre fondu

Striped bass equals European sea bass, more or less. If bass is unobtainable, substitute sea bream or red porgy – or at a pinch, fresh salmon. Phyllo pastry is available, frozen, from Greek and specialist grocers. Serves 6.

960 g/2 lb bass or similar fish
  fillets, boned and skinned
Salt and pepper
180 ml/6 fl oz/¾ cup dry white
  wine
One 15-ml spoon/1 tbs minute or
  quick-cooking tapioca
90 g/3 oz long-grain rice
Yolks of 3 hard-boiled eggs
Two 15-ml spoons/2 tbs
  finely-chopped fresh dill leaves

120–180 ml/4–6 fl oz/½–¾ cup
  melted butter
6 sheets phyllo pastry,
  approximately 35 × 40 cm/14
  × 16 in each, at room
  temperature
300 g/10 oz cold, hard butter,
  unsalted if possible, cut into
  pieces
15–30 ml/1–2 tbs lemon juice
Sprigs of fresh dill

Prepare the fish fillets and cut them into thin diagonal slices. Butter an ovenproof dish and overlap the slices across the bottom. Grind on salt and pepper, pour on wine, and cover the dish with foil. Bake at 180°C/350°F/gas mark 4 for 12–15 minutes or until the bass is cooked. Drain and reserve its liquid, let the fish cool, and drain the liquid it yields into the first quantity.

Take 90 ml/3 fl oz/a generous ⅓ cup of this, combine it with the tapioca in a small saucepan, let stand for 5 minutes, then stirring to prevent sticking, bring the mixture to a boil and simmer for 5 minutes more or until thick. Allow to drain in a fine sieve for 10 minutes.

Use the remaining bass cooking liquid – made up with water to 300 ml/½ pint/1¼ cups – to simmer the rice, tightly-covered, until all the liquid has been absorbed and the grains are tender – about 20 minutes.

Sieve the egg yolks and combine them with the rice, tapioca, and half the chopped dill. Season with salt and pepper.

Brush a large, heavy baking sheet with some of melted butter, carefully lay on it a sheet of phyllo pastry, brush the phyllo generously with melted butter, and proceed to make a stack of the 6 sheets, layering each, including the top, with butter.

Put a third of the rice mixture down the centre of the phyllo, stopping short of each end, on top of this place half the fish fillets, brush them with melted butter, and season. Add a layer of rice, the rest of the fish – buttered and seasoned – and the remaining rice. Bring together the pastry's long sides and fold over the ends to make a neat package. Brush with butter, turn it over and put the package seams-down on the baking sheet. Brush once more with butter. Bake at 190°C/375°F/gas mark 5 for 25–30 minutes, or till pastry is golden-brown.

While the parcel is in the oven, make a *beurre fondu* as follows: bring a few 15-ml spoons/tablespoons of water to the boil in a wide, heavy saucepan. Add a few pieces of hard butter, let the water boil further, and as the butter begins to melt, start whisking. Remove pan from the heat, and gradually beat in the remaining butter, returning pan to the fire three or four times as you beat. A thick, frothy emulsion will result. Whisk in lemon juice to taste and the remaining chopped dill, season and keep the sauce warm in a *bain-marie* until the pastry is cooked.

Serve the phyllo sliced on a hot platter, garnished with sprigs of dill, and pass the sauce separately.

Joan and Robert Hamilton, Honolulu Wine & Food Society, USA

King George whiting with saffron rice and chockos or other vegetables

Jack Witter describes King George whiting as one of the best Australian "eating" fish, caught in the gulfs and bays of the coasts round Victoria, South, and Western Australia. They are dark silver, slender, and usually weigh about 300 g/10 oz each. "Chockos" continue to mystify us; Jack writes that they "grow on a large green vine, . . . usually over the woodshed or other small outside building . . . are light green in colour, pear-shaped, and best eaten when very young". The recipe is for 6 people.

6 *whole whiting, King George or otherwise, weighing about 300 g/10 oz each, cleaned and gutted, heads and tails intact*	120 *g/4 oz butter*
	360 *g/12 oz long-grain rice*
	A 1.25-ml spoon/¼ teasp powdered saffron
4 *cloves garlic*	*Pepper*
Salt	*Young green pawpaw, young chockos, small cucumbers, or small marrows*
240 *ml/8 fl oz/1 cup dry white wine*	

Wash and dry the fish, rub them with peeled garlic and salt. Finely chop the garlic cloves, strew them into a sizeable but shallow baking dish with 30 g/1 oz butter. Place the fish, split side down and curved into a semi-circle, inside the dish, pour on the wine, cover tightly with foil and bake in a 180°C/350°F/gas mark 4 oven for about 20 minutes or until the fish are done.

Meanwhile boil the rice in salted water for 20 minutes or until cooked. Dissolve the saffron in a very little boiling water, drain the rice if necessary, fluff it, add the saffron, 30 g/1 oz butter, and seasoning. Mound into the middle of a large serving plate and keep hot.

Remove the cooked fish from their dish and keep them similarly hot while reducing the cooking liquid over a high heat until enough remains to sauce the whiting. Over the same heat, whisk in 60 g/2 oz butter, 15 g/½ oz at a time; the butter will give the stock a liaison. Check seasoning and strain.

Arrange the fish with their heads perched atop the rice and their tails curved around the plate. Serve with the sauce in a warmed boat and pass as vegetables the peeled pawpaw sliced and steamed, or chockos, cucumbers, or marrows treated in the same fashion.

J. A. Witter, New South Wales Wine & Food Society, Australia

Tahini sauce for fish

Based on *tahini* or sesame paste, available from Middle Eastern or specialist grocers, this is successful in small quantities with assertive fish like grilled mackerel or swordfish. Serves 4–6.

75 g/2½ oz tahini paste
1 large clove garlic, peeled and
  broken down with salt
Juice of 1 lemon

90–120 ml/3–4 fl oz/⅜–½ cup
  water
Salt and pepper
Two 15-ml spoons/2 tbs chopped
  parsley

In the bowl of a blender or food processor, blend the first three ingredients, the lesser quantity of water, and seasoning. Add more water if necessary to loosen consistency, taste for salt and pepper, stir in parsley.

Can be made several hours ahead and refrigerated, covered. Bring the sauce to room temperature to serve.

Karen Celeste Aborjaily, Boston Wine & Food Society, USA

Porc d'amour

Serves 6.

240 g/8 oz thinly-sliced onions
3 large cloves garlic
Oil and butter
12 juniper berries
Salt and pepper
1½ kg/3¼ lb boned and rindless loin
  of pork with most of the fat
  removed

360 ml/12 fl oz/1½ cups light red
  wine
90 g/3 oz concentrated tomato
  paste
A good pinch each of dried thyme
  and oregano
Boiled, buttered noodles

Sweat the onions and peeled, minced garlic in a little oil and butter until soft and transluscent but not browning. Remove from the heat, add the juniper berries, slightly crushed, some salt and pepper, mix and cool.

Open the pork, boned side up, salt and pepper it, and spread half the onion mixture down the centre of the meat. Roll and tie the loin with white butchers' string at 2½ cm/1 in intervals, and tie the ends. Dry the meat and season the outside. Heat 30 g/1 oz butter with a little oil in a heavy casserole or cocotte, oval if possible and just big enough to contain the pork, and brown the meat lightly on all sides. Pour out most of the fat, wipe the cocotte of any burned butter, and return the loin to it. Add the remaining onion and juniper, the wine, tomato, and herbs, plus a little salt.

Cover the cocotte with a double layer of foil, put the lid on, and braise the meat at 155°C/310°F/gas mark 2 in the lower middle of the oven for about 2 hours – turning the loin over once – or until a meat thermometer reads 82°C/180°F when inserted into the centre of the loin.

Let the pork rest for 20 minutes on a hot platter. Degrease the casserole juices, reduce them to a good consistency, correct seasoning, strain, and reheat. Cut string from the meat, carve it, and serve with hot buttered noodles and the just-made sauce.

Colin Reynolds, Stockport, Cheshire, England

Sheep's head pie

Another "old family recipe" from Anne Kidd, who says that "claret is the traditional accompaniment". Serves 6.

Rough puff pastry

240 g/8 oz/generous 1½ cups plain   180 g/6 oz chilled butter
    flour   About 45 ml/3 tbs iced water
A small pinch of salt

Filling

1 skinned sheep's head or 2   2 hard-boiled eggs
    skinned lambs' heads   2 slices rindless bacon, uncooked
Salt   Chopped parsley
1 pig or calf's foot, bone removed,   A pinch dried rosemary
    foot split lengthwise   1 egg yolk
A good pinch each grated nutmeg
    (or ground mace) and ground
    ginger

Make the rough-puff the night before you need it. Sift the flour and salt into a bowl, cut the butter into cubes and use a pair of knives to cut them into the flour until thoroughly integrated. Add just under 45 ml/3 tbs iced water, bring the dough together with your hands, add a little more water if necessary to make the pastry adhere without becoming damp, form a ball and chill it, wrapped in greaseproof or waxed paper, for half an hour.

Then roll the dough on a floured board into a rectangle, fold it from top to bottom into three like a business letter, turn it 90° so that an open end of the "letter" is towards you, roll it again into a rectangle, fold it into three once more, wrap and chill it for half an hour. Repeat the rolling and folding twice more, wrap the pastry airtight and chill it.

Steep the head(s) in salted water overnight to draw their blood. Split them and remove the brains (for use, perhaps, in brain cakes, page 184). Put heads into a large pot, cover with cold water, add the pig's or calf's foot, bring water to the boil and skim it thoroughly. Turn the heat down, add salt and spices and simmer the heads, half-covered with a lid, for about 2 hours or until the flesh comes easily from the bones. Let cool somewhat in the broth, remove the heads, pick meat from the bones and cut it into small pieces. Peel and thinly slice the tongues, and discard the foot.

Layer meat and tongues with sliced eggs and cut-up bacon in a rimmed pie dish of medium size. Season, strew with chopped parsley and a very little rosemary. Fill the dish with part of the strained broth (use the rest for soup), leave it to set a bit, and brush the dish's rim with some of the egg yolk beaten in a little water. Roll out the pastry and run a strip of it around this. Cover the dish with more pastry, press it with a fork round the rim, brush with the egg-wash, refrigerate for half an hour, and cut steam vents in the top.

Bake the pie for 20 minutes at 230°C/450°F/gas mark 8, turn the oven down to 190°C/375°F/gas mark 5 for a further 20–25 minutes. Remove, cool, and serve cold with salads; the filling will jell nicely, due to the foot's gelatine.

Ann Kidd, East Lothian, Scotland

Oriental-style barbecued chicken

These we didn't barbecue, but baked in the oven as alternatively directed, and found them tasty and very tender. Serves 8.

120 g/4 oz finely-chopped spring onions (scallions)	120 ml/4 fl oz/½ cup dark soy sauce
60 ml/4 tbs peanut oil	45 ml/3 tbs honey
3 cloves garlic	30 ml/2 tbs sesame oil
1½ × 5-ml spoons/1½ teasp peeled, grated fresh ginger root	Two 1½ kg/3¼ lb fresh chickens, each cut into 4 serving pieces
	Pepper

Heat the onions in peanut oil; add the peeled and chopped garlic, ginger, soy sauce, and honey, bring these to the boil. Remove from the heat, add sesame oil and mix.

Lightly oil the chicken pieces and brown them briefly on both sides on the grill of a barbecue or under a broiler – or "grill" in the British sense. Grind on pepper and put each piece onto a double thickness of aluminium foil just big enough to make up an individual parcel, divide the sauce among these, and seal the parcels by rolling the edges tightly. Place on the grill of a barbecue, cover, and bake for 15–20 minutes. If the grill lacks a cover, the cooking will take longer.

Alternatively, bake the parcels for 25 minutes in a 190°C/375°F/gas mark 5 oven.

Serve the chicken in or out of its foil, with sauce in abundance.

Sue Hinsdale, Palm Beach, Florida Wine & Food Society, USA

Burmese chicken

A rich and delicate dish which should not be served with assertive partners. *Masala* means a mixture of spices, and, if absolutely necessary, vegetable oil can be substituted for *ghee*. Serves 6–8.

Masala

60 g/2 oz each creamed coconut
  and blanched pistachios
120 g/4 oz each blanched almonds
  and raisins
Seeds of 7 cardamom pods
7 cloves
5 fresh red chili peppers, seeded

1 stick cinnamon
One 15-ml spoon/1 tbs white
  poppy seeds
One 5-ml spoon/1 teasp ground
  cumin
One 2.5-ml spoon/½ teasp ground
  turmeric

To finish

3 large onions
One 2½ cm/1 in piece of fresh
  ginger root
4 cloves garlic
Salt
180 g/6 oz ghee

1 large fresh oven-ready chicken
150 ml/5 fl oz/scant ⅔ cup each
  plain yoghurt and thick cream
A squeeze of lemon juice
Plain boiled long-grain rice

Mix ingredients of the *masala* and grind them – using an electric coffee mill, if possible – in small quantities to a smooth paste, adding up to as much as 300 ml/½ pint/1¼ cups water as you do so.

Peel and finely chop the onions. Scrape the papery skin from the ginger root and grate it. Peel the garlic and with the aid of salt, mash it to a paste. Melt half the *ghee* in a large sauté pan and soften these ingredients, covered, over a very low heat, stirring occasionally, for about 45 minutes. Take care not to let them brown.

Cut the chicken, on the bone, into 16–20 pieces.

In a second large sauté pan, melt the remaining *ghee* and cook the *masala* without allowing it to brown, turning the mixture constantly with a wooden spoon. Eventually it will form a cohesive mass and begin to look oily. Remove from the pan and let it cool on a plate so as not to brown in the pan's residual heat.

When the onion mixture is ready, add the cut-up thigh and drumstick meat, 150 ml/5 fl oz/scant ⅔ cup water, one 5-ml spoon/1 teasp salt. Bring these to the boil, reduce heat, and cover pan with a tight-fitting lid. Simmer over a low heat for about 15 minutes, then add the remaining chicken. Continue cooking, covered, until all the chicken is tender – about 15–20 minutes more.

Stir in the *masala* and gently bring all back to the boil. Simmer uncovered for about 5 minutes; the liquid will reduce and the mixture swell. Add the yoghurt, cream, and lemon juice, stir, reduce if necessary to achieve a good consistency, test seasoning and serve with plain boiled rice.

Jenny Kavarana, Surrey, England

Codornices "à la maître d'hôtel" con pimientos verdes y rojos

A marriage between Spanish – or is it Mexican? – and French, linking quail with sweet peppers and parsley butter. Serves 6.

2 each sweet green and red peppers	6 quail
90 g/3 oz black olives, weighed	2 large cloves garlic
after stoning	Parsley stalks
2 lemons	Salt and pepper
Olive oil	

Roast the peppers under a grill or broiler until the skin blisters and blackens and the flesh has cooked. Remove, and when cool enough to handle, lift away the skin, open peppers and remove the seeds, slice the flesh lengthwise into thin strips. Chop the olives and put them, with the peppers, into a china bowl with the juice of 1 lemon – plus a little olive oil – to marinate for several hours.

Split the quail down the back, remove backbones, and flatten the birds. Marinate for an hour in a few spoonfuls of olive oil, juice of the other lemon, peeled and chopped garlic, and a few parsley stalks.

When ready to go, shake excess marinade from the quail, season them well, and grill or broil on both sides for a total of 15–20 minutes, basting frequently with their marinade, until they test done.

Drain and season the peppers and olives, heat them through and serve with the quail as a sort of vegetable garnish. Let a few slices of *salsa* "à la maître d'hôtel" melt over each quail as you present it.

Salsa "à la maître d'hôtel"

180 g/6 oz butter, softened
15 ml/1 tbs lemon juice

Three 15-ml spoons/3 tbs chopped
    parsley
Salt and pepper

Cream the butter in a bowl with a wooden spoon till very, very light. Gradually beat in the lemon juice, followed by parsley, and salt and pepper to taste. Roll the butter into a cylinder, wrap in foil, and refrigerate till hard. Remove the foil and slice to serve.

Dr. Leopold S. Tuchman, Hollywood, California Wine & Food
Society, USA

Pheasant in brandy sauce

Serves 6.

2 plump oven-ready pheasant,
    never frozen, both of the same
    sex
360 ml/12 fl oz/1½ cups full-bodied
    red wine
180 ml/6 fl oz/¾ cup brandy
½ lemon
Salt
60 g/2 oz butter

A few slices of fatty bacon
600 ml/1 pint/2½ cups game stock,
    made as for chicken broth on
    page 219, but using a pheasant
    carcass, less water, and a
    shorter simmering time
Six 15-ml spoons/6 tbs each red
    currant jelly and French
    mustard, Dijon if possible
Pepper

Watercress and bacon rolls as garnish

Cut the birds in half lengthwise and trim away their backbones, reserving these for the sauce. Clean the pheasants' insides under cold running water and pat them dry. If you suspect that the birds are old or not well-hung, marinate the pieces in the wine, brandy, and juice of the half-lemon for a day or two to tenderise. It's probably advisable to do this anyway.

Dry the birds of their excess marinade, salt them, and smear all over with the butter. Lay the pieces side by side and skin side up in a heavy casserole or cocotte into which they will just fit. Lay over them the fatty bacon, and roast, uncovered, for 10 minutes at 220°C/425°F/gas mark

7. Cover the pieces closely with a double layer of buttered greaseproof or parchment paper, tucked well down over them, and put the lid on the casserole. Lower the oven to 165°C/325°F/gas mark 3, and cook for another 1½ hours or until the pheasant are tender. This will depend on the age and sex of the birds, length of hanging, and whether they are marinated. If legs pull easily from the body, they should be done.

Towards the end of roasting time, put the liquid from the marinade into a saucepan with the stock and backbones. Boil over a high heat until reduced by half, remove the bones, whisk in the jelly and mustard and reduce further, simmering gently, until you have a rich, syrupy sauce. Season, and judge whether to add more red currant or mustard to balance the flavours.

Remove the pheasant from their cocotte and let them rest in a warm place for about 10 minutes. Carefully pour the fat from the casserole, leaving the brown drippings, add the sauce and let it simmer while you scrape in the drippings as the liquid bubbles. Remove bacon from the birds and carve the meat onto a hot platter. If necessary, cover the platter with a wet and wrung-out tea-towel and reheat under the grill or broiler until the towel begins to steam. Pour on a bit of the sauce and serve the rest in a heated boat.

Garnish the platter with watercress, plus bacon rolls made by rolling up strips of rindless streaky or belly bacon, fastening them with wooden toothpicks, and grilling them gently until quite crisp. Remove the toothpicks and serve hot.

Jenny Kavarana, Surrey, England

Bawd bree

In English, "Scots hare soup". Serves 6.

1 hare	parsley, thyme, tied into a
15 ml/1 tbs vinegar	bunch)
1 piece of beef shin (fore shank),	Salt
cut into two	A good pinch of mixed spice
2 medium onions, peeled and stuck	6 black peppercorns
with cloves	A handful of medium or "middle"
2 medium carrots	oatmeal
1 small turnip	Ground pepper if necessary
3 celery stalks	Port
A bouquet garni (bay leaf,	Boiled potatoes

Ask your butcher to skin and cut up a hare and to save the blood in a jar. Add vinegar to prevent the blood curdling, and hold this in the refrigerator.

Wipe the hare's joints with a damp cloth to remove small hairs, and put the pieces, with the beef shin or shank, into a large pot or saucepan. Cover well with cold water, and bring to the boil. Skim thoroughly.

Add the onions, the peeled carrots and turnip, the celery, *bouquet garni*, salt, and spices. Simmer gently for 4 hours, half-covered, adding the peppercorns during the last half-hour of cooking.

Strain the resultant stock, discard the beef, vegetables, herbs, and pepper, pick the hare meat from its bones, and purée it in a blender or food processor, adding enough stock to constitute a soup. Return this to the cleaned pan, gradually add the oatmeal, stirring as you do so, and cook slowly for 1 hour, stirring frequently. Thin with more stock if necessary.

Strain the hare's blood, whisk in a few spoonfuls of the soup to heat it, then beat this back into the rest, "in one direction only", and let it cook, below the boiling point, for 10 minutes, while continuing to stir. Blood, being protein, will curdle if boiled.

Judge seasoning and add a little port to taste. "Plain boiled potatoes are always served with hare soup," says the contributor.

Anne Kidd, East Lothian, Scotland

Short and savoury

Kidneys with calvados and cream

Serves 2 as a little supper dish.

5 fresh lambs' kidneys
Salt and pepper
Oil
45 ml/3 tbs calvados
120–150 ml/4–5 fl oz/½–⅔ cup
  thick cream

About one 5-ml spoon/1 teasp
  French mustard, preferably
  Dijon
Chopped parsley

Remove fat from the kidneys, peel off their membranes, split, and cut away the fatty cores. Slice into bite-sized pieces and season.

Heat a heavy sauté pan, add a film of oil, and when very hot, toss in the kidneys. Cook them quickly, tossing often, for a very few minutes, until they are well-done on the outside and rare and melting within. Drain them onto a hot plate and keep warm in a low oven.

Wipe the pan, pour in the calvados, flame it, and let reduce over a brisk heat to about 15 ml/1 tbs. Add cream, reduce it until thickened and sufficient to coat the kidneys without great excess, add a touch of mustard to taste, season, and return kidneys, drained of their exuded blood, to the sauce. Stir well and taste again for seasoning.

Spoon onto hot plates, garnish with parsley, and rush to the table.

Joy Fontes Rothwell, Manchester Wine & Food Society, England and
Houston Wine & Food Society, Texas, USA

Mushrooms with kidneys and leeks

Another supper dish with kidneys, not as rich as Joy Rothwell's, but quite filling. Len Evans, Australia's best-known wineman, suggests finishing the sauce with a little *demi-glace*, but as few domestic cooks are likely to have this to hand, we've substituted a swirl of butter and wine vinegar. Serves 4.

8–12 flat mushrooms, each about
   8 cm/3 in diameter
150 g/5 oz butter
Salt and pepper
6 slim leeks

8 fresh lambs' or 3 veal kidneys
Oil
A flavoured wine vinegar
Good whole meal or whole wheat
   bread

Wash and dry the mushrooms, cut off their stalks, melt half the butter and brush both sides of the fungi with this. Place them, stem side up, on a big rack above a tin for roasting meat.

Wash and trim the leeks, slice the white part and some of the green into thin rings. Prepare the kidneys as in the previous recipe and cut them into bite-sized pieces.

Place mushrooms, with their roasting tin, into a 180°C/350°F/gas mark 4 oven and bake for 10–12 minutes until cooked but still firm. They will give off a lot of juice which can be used in soup.

Meanwhile sweat the leeks with 15 g/½ oz butter and some salt and pepper in a covered saucepan until tender – about 5 minutes. Hold, covered, until ready to use.

Sauté the kidneys as in the previous recipe.

Working fast, divide the mushrooms, stem side up and well-drained, among four hot plates, strew on the drained leeks and kidneys. Season further if you think necessary. Melt the remaining butter, quickly, in a small saucepan, and as it bubbles, add a good dash of vinegar. Pour this, swirling, onto the food.

Eat with plenty of bread to mop up the sauce and tasty juices.

Len Evans, Sydney, New South Wales, Australia

Gratin of artichoke hearts

Serves 10, for lunch, with salad.

2 jars, weighing 180–210 g/6–7 oz
each, of artichoke hearts in oil
15 g/½ oz butter
120 g/4 oz finely-chopped spring
onions (scallions)
2 large cloves garlic
Salt and pepper
180 g/6 oz Gruyère or similar
cheese
5 whole eggs

2–3 egg yolks
480 ml/16 fl oz/2 cups cream
A handful chopped parsley and
watercress, mixed
Grated Parmesan cheese
Optional: shredded cooked chicken,
or 30 g/1 oz coarsely-chopped
walnuts lightly browned in
butter

Remove artichoke hearts from oil and slice them thin. Heat a little of the same oil, with butter, in a heavy sauté pan and sweat the onions and peeled, minced garlic until soft. Add the artichokes and sauté them to colour slightly. Season well with salt and pepper.

Butter two shallow baking or gratin dishes of 23 cm/9 in each in diameter and divide the allium-artichoke mixture between them, spreading it round. Grate the Gruyère and strew it on.

Whisk together the eggs, yolks, cream, parsley and watercress, salt and pepper and pour this over the artichokes.

Bake the dishes at 190°C/375°F/gas mark 5 for 30–40 minutes or until the gratins are puffed and golden. Sprinkle on a little grated Parmesan, slice, and serve.

The chicken or walnuts can be seasoned and added to the artichokes, etc. before the Gruyère, if you like.

Barbara D. Holland, Columbus, Ohio Wine & Food Society, USA

Grandfather's egg

"My grandfather made this as a treat for nursery tea when he came to visit," says Pat Matthews, who recommends it as a rapid lunch. Serves 1.

1 *or* 2 *eggs*   1 *or* 2 *slices of bread*
A *large knob of butter*   *Salt and pepper*

Soft boil the egg(s) – which will probably take about 3½ minutes from room temperature – and warm a pudding basin or small, pretty bowl. Drop in the butter, peel the eggs while still hot and scoop them into the bowl. Take crusts off the bread, crumble it into the egg and butter and mix well. Add salt and pepper to taste. The result should be firm; if not, add more bread and mix again.

Patrick Matthews, London, England

Vegetables and a salad

Aubergine l'auberge

We love these on their own. Bonnie McConnell recommends them with meat, and the gardener of page 26 will have ample ingredients. The anchovy fillets are our addition. Serves 6.

2 long, slim, and very firm
   aubergines (egg-plants),
   weighing a total of 420 g/14 oz
Salt
Oil
2 cloves garlic
480 g/1 lb fresh tomatoes or the
   same weight of canned plum
   tomatoes, with their juices

Two 5-ml spoons/2 teasp
   granulated sugar
Big pinch of dried basil
Pepper
About 180 g/6 oz mild cheese like
   mozzarella
A small can of anchovy fillets
Fresh basil and chopped parsley

Wash the aubergines and cut them across, with skins on, into slices a scant 1½ cm/½ in thick – there should be about 20 of these. Salt them liberally, place in single layers on plates, stack the plates one atop the other and cover the top layer with a weighted dish. Leave for 45 minutes. Press out the bitter juices, wash and dry the slices thoroughly.

Lightly paint them with oil and grill or broil each side under a hot flame or element until tender and browning. Set aside.

Run a thin film of oil into a medium sauté pan, put in the peeled and minced garlic, sauté briefly and add the peeled and seeded tomatoes or canned tomatoes and their juices, the sugar, dried basil, and a good pinch of salt. Break up the tomatoes with a wooden spoon and cook the mixture over a brisk heat, stirring frequently, until it's reduced to a very concentrated purée. Add pepper and judge the seasoning, which should be quite savoury.

Slice the cheese very thin, dry a few anchovy fillets of their excess oil and cut each into 2 or 3 strips. Divide the tomato sauce among the aubergine slices, just to cover, top each with a slice of mozzarella cut to fit, and a criss-cross of anchovy. Bake these on a lightly-oiled sheet at 165°C/325°F/gas mark 3 for 10–15 minutes, or until the cheese is melting and the aubergine is hot through.

Garnish each piece with scissored basil leaves, if available, and chopped parsley. Serve several slices per person.

Bonnie McConnell, Northern Illinois Wine & Food Society, USA

Gootsie's carrot casserole

Serves 8.

720 g/1½ lb peeled, diced carrots
One 15-ml spoon/1 tbs caraway
  seeds
A pinch of granulated sugar
Salt
90 g/3 oz butter

75 g/2½ oz peeled, finely-chopped
  onion
160 ml/generous 5 fl oz/⅔ cup
  meat broth (page 220)
60 g/2 oz fresh breadcrumbs
Pepper
120 g/4 oz grated Cheddar or
  equivalent cheese

Place the carrots and caraway seeds in a large saucepan and cover them with water. Add a pinch of sugar and a dash of salt. Bring all to the boil and simmer for 10–20 minutes – depending on the carrots' age – until they're just tender. Drain well. Butter a casserole of 2¾ litres/5 pints/3 quarts capacity and put in the carrots, minus most of the carraway.

Melt 30 g/1 oz of the butter and sweat the onions in it over a low heat until they brown lightly. Stir in the broth and add all to the carrots.

Melt the remaining butter and mix it with the breadcrumbs, a 5-ml spoon/1 teasp salt, a little pepper, and the grated cheese. Spread this evenly over the carrots and onions and bake the casserole, uncovered, at 180°C/350°F/gas mark 4 for 30 minutes.

Perrine Palmer, Miami, Florida Wine & Food Society, USA

Champagne cabbage

Barbara Holland specifies champagne, but any good-quality dry sparkling wine will do. Serves 8–10.

2 large onions
60 g/2 oz butter
3 large tart apples
1 red cabbage and 1 green one,
    each weighing about 480 g/1 lb
360 ml/12 fl oz/1½ cups
    champagne or similar wine, at
    room temperature

30 g/2 tbs granulated sugar
One 5-ml spoon/1 teasp each
    grated lemon zest and salt
30 ml/2 tbs lemon juice
Pepper

Peel and slice the onions very thin. In a deep flameproof casserole or large heavy saucepan melt the butter and sweat the onions until they soften.

Quarter, pare, and core the apples, cut them into ½ cm/⅛ in slices, add to the onions and sauté for 5 minutes.

Core the cabbage and cut them very, very thin. Add to the casserole with a third of the champagne, the sugar, lemon zest, salt, and lemon juice. Bring to the boil and simmer gently, covered, for 15 minutes. Add the remaining champagne and some pepper and simmer, uncovered, for 10 minutes more. Serve at once.

The acid in the champagne and lemon will crisp the cabbage.

Barbara D. Holland, Columbus, Ohio Wine & Food Society, USA

Savoury pumpkin

Serves 6.

1½ kg/3¼ lb pumpkin flesh
Salt
Butter

Cream
Worcestershire sauce
Pepper

Cut the pumpkin into cubes and boil these in salted water until tender. Drain very well, and while still hot, mash to a purée. Turn the purée over a low heat with a knob of butter to dry it – this is a very watery vegetable – add some cream, a little Worcestershire sauce, and pepper to taste. Salt further if necessary. Serve very hot.

Peter C. Joyce, Victoria Wine & Food Society, Australia

Sweet-sour beans

Conceived as a salad for the local Wine & Food Society picnic, this serves 8–10 people.

960 g/2 lb green French beans
Salt
180 g/6 oz lean bacon
15 ml/1 tbs oil
2 medium onions

45 g/2½ tbs granulated sugar
240 ml/8 fl oz/1 cup cider or wine
  vinegar
Pepper

Top, tail, and if necessary string the beans and boil them in salted water for 2–10 minutes – depending on beans' age and size – until just tender. Drain and refresh them in very cold water, drain and dry thoroughly.

If need be, remove rinds from the bacon and chop it fine. Sauté in oil for 2–3 minutes. Mince the peeled onions very fine, add them to the bacon, cover and sweat for 5 minutes. Stir in the sugar and vinegar and simmer, uncovered, for 10 minutes more.

Pour this over the beans, add salt and pepper and mix well. When cool, refrigerate overnight, stirring beans often in their marinade. The acid will crisp and turn them khaki colour.

Serve the beans as a salad, drained of excess vinegar.

Audrey Wilkerson, Cotswold Wine & Food Society, England, and wife of former Chairman, Joe Wilkerson

Desserts and a shortbread

Pink champagne sorbet

Fragrant, delicate, and quite different from our palate-cleansing *crémant* sorbet of page 65, this calls for cream and an orange liqueur. Serves 6–8.

240 ml/8 fl oz/1 cup thick cream
210 g/7 oz/1 cup castor
  (granulated) sugar
600 ml/1 pint/2½ cups chilled

rosé champagne or similar dry,
  pink méthode champenoise wine
2 egg whites
60 ml/4 tbs orange liqueur

Combine the cream and ¾ of the sugar in a heavy saucepan. Stir the mixture over a low heat to dissolve the sugar. Cool, beat to reintegrate, and whisk in the champagne. Pour this into a deep plastic box or metal container, cover with a lid and freeze for several hours until semi-frozen. Beat the egg whites to stiff, then gradually whisk in remaining sugar until the peaks shine.

Turn the sorbet base into a food processor, add the orange liqueur, and whirl them together. Pour this onto the whites and fold the two deftly but thoroughly into one.

Return to the container and refreeze. We found that because of the strength of its alcohol the sorbet did not become very hard – not necessarily a disadvantage, but a preparation for fast melting.

Spoon the sorbet into glasses frosted in the freezer, and serve immediately.

As for other wine-based ices, make this one 36–48 hours in advance of eating, since alcohol delays the freezing process.

Richard S. Webster, Northern Illinois Wine & Food Society, USA

Sally Lunn with chocolate mousse, custard sauce

This is a combination of two recipes already given, and serves 4.

Take one of the three Sally Lunns set out on page 135, carefully cut a large triangular lid from the top, wrap the lid in a tea-towel and store it to keep fresh. Make a chocolate mousse as for the black bottom pies on page 168, using:

150 g/5 oz semi-sweet chocolate
75 g/2½ oz butter, unsalted if
* possible*
2.5 g/½ teasp powdered gelatine, or
* ½ leaf European gelatine*

Dark rum
2 eggs
1 egg white
One 15-ml spoon/1 tbs icing
* (confectioners') sugar*

The extra egg white makes this mousse a bit lighter than its model, and should be whisked with the other whites as in the prototype recipe.

When the mousse is ready, carefully cut and scoop out enough crumb from the Sally Lunn to make a cavity that takes the mousse – do this evenly, as haphazard cutting will be revealed when the dessert is sliced! Put the crumbs aside for another use, pile in the mousse, give the top a swirl, and chill the result – low in the refrigerator and covered with a bowl to keep moisture in and smells out – for several hours to set the chocolate.

Remove from the cold about 30 minutes before serving and present Sally Lunn with her lid set at a jaunty angle. Remove the lid and slice the dessert with a heated knife. Serve with the following custard.

Custard
360 ml/12 fl oz/1½ cups milk
1 split vanilla bean
5 egg yolks

90 g/3 oz/scant ½ cup castor
* (granulated) sugar*
Kirsch

Infuse the milk with vanilla bean in a very heavy saucepan while beating the yolks and sugar until very thick and light. When the milk has reached the scalding point, remove it from the heat, take out the vanilla, and pour slowly onto the yolks and sugar, beating fast. Sieve this back into the milk pan. Over a high heat, whisk vigorously, bringing the custard up to the first boil. This happens quickly; the mixture suddenly thickens and you must immediately sieve it into a chilled bowl to prevent curdling. Beat to cool rapidly, add a little kirsch to sharpen the flavour. A custard like this, rich in egg yolks, *can* be boiled, but only just.

When cool, chill thoroughly and serve in a jug or pitcher.

Crêpes Suzette

Serves 8.

Crêpes

190 g/generous 6 oz/generous 1¼   3 eggs
  cups plain flour   390 ml/13 fl oz/scant 1⅔ cups milk
Pinch of salt   30 ml/2 tbs melted and cooled
Two 5-ml spoons/2 teasp castor   butter
  (granulated) sugar   Oil

Sauce

10 sugar lumps   75 ml/5 tbs triple sec curaçao
2 small oranges   150 ml/5 fl oz/a scant ⅔ cup each
1 lemon   brandy and Grand Marnier
90 g/3 oz butter, unsalted if
  possible

Either make the *crêpe* batter by putting all of its ingredients into a blender, blending for 6 seconds, scraping down the sides with a rubber spatula and reblending for half a minute, *or* sift the dry ingredients together into a bowl, make a well in the centre and break in the eggs. Carefully whisk the eggs into the flour, moving from the centre out, while adding half the milk. Beat vigorously to combine as thoroughly as possible, beat in the remaining milk, sieve the mixture to eliminate any lingering lumps, add the butter.

If using the blender, pour the finished batter into a bowl, and either way cover the bowl with a cloth and let the contents rest for 2 hours.

To make the *crêpes*, take a heavy, seasoned *crêpe* pan of about 14½ cm/5½ in across the base, warm it over a medium heat until a drop of water sizzles and evaporates on contact. Brush on a drop of oil, stir the batter, and ladle in about 30 ml/2 tbs of this, turning the pan fast until the batter covers the bottom. Quickly tip away any excess; the *crêpes* should be ultra-thin.

Cook until the *crêpe's* upper surface looks dry and the edges begin to curl – anywhere from 20–60 seconds. Free these with a palette knife, and flip the pancake over. Cook – less than a minute – until the underside is golden. Slip the *crêpe* onto a plate. Wipe the pan with an oiled paper if you think necessary (though this probably need not happen between each *crêpe*) and proceed until all the batter has been used, stirring every time. Stack the *crêpes*, when cool, on a plate, cover and hold them at room temperature. Or, if made a day in advance, wrap in plastic, refrigerate, and return them to room temperature before use.

To start the sauce, rub half the sugar lumps over the skin of 1 orange and the rest over the lemon until all are soaked with the citrus oils. Use the lemon for something else, but squeeze and strain the juice of both oranges.

The dish will be finished in flames, at the table. Take each *crêpe*, fold it in half and in half again to form a triangle, and bring all the triangles on a plate to the table with the sugar lumps, orange juice, butter, and the combined liqueurs.

Light the burner of a chafing dish and set over it a wide pan. Put the sugar cubes into the pan, crush them with a fork as they heat, gradually add the orange juice and allow it to simmer. Add the butter and stir with a fork until the mixture reduces slightly and becomes creamy. Plunge in the folded *crêpes*, heat them, turning once, carefully pour in the liqueurs and if they don't flame immediately, light them with a match. Gently move the pan over the heat until the flames are extinguished, and serve the folded *crêpes*, generously sauced, without delay.

Lindsay Karnovsky, Johannesburg Wine & Food Society, South Africa

Princess rhubarb, custard sauce

Joan Chenhalls makes this with forced rhubarb, which is hot-house grown and available in England from Christmas week until February or

March. The strands are thin and bright pink, and Joan usually buys it by
the yard! The dessert, refreshingly tart, serves 4.

480 g/1 lb forced rhubarb
120 g/4 oz/generous ½ cup
  granulated sugar

15 g/½ oz powdered gelatine, or 4
  leaves European gelatine
Grated zest and juice of 1 lemon
2 eggs

Cut the rhubarb into short lengths and place these in a heavy,
non-aluminium saucepan with 30 g/1 oz sugar and several tablespoons
of water. Cook the stalks covered, over a very low heat until soft and
yielding their juice.

Sieve the juice into a bowl, pressing the rhubarb hard to extract all of
its liquid and flavour; you should have 600 ml/1 pint/2½ cups juice.
Discard the pulp, pour the juice into a saucepan, add the gelatine, let
soften, and dissolve it, swirling the pan, over a low heat, add and
dissolve the remaining sugar, stir in the lemon zest and strained juice.
Remove from the heat and allow to cool.

Oil a mould of about 1200 ml/2 pints/5 cups capacity, separate the
eggs (reserving yolks for the custard), and when the rhubarb mixture is
cold and near the setting point, whisk the whites to peaks and fold all
together. Turn into the mould and refrigerate for several hours or
overnight.

To serve, dip the mould briefly into hot water and turn out the
dessert; serve it with a chilled pouring custard based on the leftover
yolks, plus 3 additional yolks and the sugar, milk, vanilla, and kirsch as
set out and described on pages 213–14.

Joan Chenhalls, London branch, England

Strawberry and chocolate tart

Strawberries and chocolate, with pastry cream in the middle. Serves 6.

Half-quantity shortcrust II, page
  222
180 ml/6 fl oz/¾ cup milk
1 split vanilla bean
2 egg yolks

A generous 45 g/3 tbs castor
  (granulated) sugar
⅔ × 15-ml spoon/⅔ tbs each plain
  flour and potato flour or
  cornflour (cornstarch)

30 ml/2 tbs thick cream
Kirsch
60 g/2 oz semi-sweet chocolate

360–480 g/12–16 oz ripe
strawberries, as uniform in size
as possible
Four 15-ml spoons/4 tbs red
currant jelly

Roll out the shortcrust pastry and use it to line a 23 cm/9 in flan ring set onto a heavy baking sheet. Refrigerate to relax the dough for half an hour, and bake it blind, lined with greaseproof or parchment paper weighted with dried beans or coins, in a 190°C/375°F/gas mark 5 oven for about 20–25 minutes – removing paper when the pastry has set – or until golden and browning. Cool completely.

Meanwhile, make the pastry cream. Bring the milk to the scalding point with the vanilla bean while beating the yolks with the sugar until thick. Sift the 2 flours (potato or cornflour makes for lighter pastry cream) onto the yolks, beat well, pour on the milk through a sieve, whisk together, and pour the mixture into a small, heavy saucepan. Over a very low heat, whisk the pastry cream until it thickens and boils, beating vigorously to avoid the slightest lump. Boil for 30 seconds, whisking, and turn the cream onto a plate. Cover the top with plastic wrap to prevent the formation of skin, and cool completely.

Melt the chocolate in a *bain-marie*, and with a palette knife, spread it evenly over the bottom of the cooled tart shell. Refrigerate for about 10 minutes to set.

When the pastry cream is cold, put it into a small bowl and beat to aerate it. With a small fork, half-whip the cream, whisk in a few drops of kirsch, and beat this into the pastry cream until completely smooth and light. If there is even a suspicion of lump, pass the mixture through a fine sieve.

Spread 240 g/8 oz of this over the base of the chocolate-covered tart shell, and use the remaining dollop elsewhere.

Carefully pull – not cut – stems from the strawberries, halve them lengthwise, and arrange the halves, right side out and overlapping, round the outside of the tart, working your way in diminishing circles to the centre until no pastry cream is visible.

Simmer the jelly for a minute or two with a dash of kirsch, then take a pastry brush and deftly paint all the strawberries with jelly, being careful not to let it drip down into the cream.

The tart should be eaten within 2 hours of assembly.

Shortbread cookies

An extremely speedy, "short", and very light version. Makes 6–7 dozen.

480 g/1 lb very soft butter,
    preferably unsalted
450 g/15 oz/3 cups plain flour
A pinch of salt, if butter is
    unsalted

150 g/5 oz/1 cup icing
    (confectioners') sugar
90 g/3 oz/½ cup cornflour
    (cornstarch)

Put the butter into a large bowl, sift in the flour and salt (if salt is used), followed by sugar and cornflour (cornstarch), both sifted. Whip for 5 minutes with an electric beater at high speed. Drop the batter by 5-ml spoons/teaspoonfuls onto heavy baking sheets, lightly buttered, and bake at 165°C/325°F/gas mark 3 for 25 minutes. Don't allow the cookies to brown.

Cool on racks and store in airtight tins.

Elizabeth Charpie, Boston Wine & Food Society, USA

A few basics

Three basic broths for soups and sauces

Chicken broth
To make about 1¾ litres/3 pints/2 quarts.

720 g/1½ lb fresh chicken pieces
2 carrots
1 each onion and celery stalk
6 or so parsley stalks

1 bay leaf
Pinch dried thyme
One 2.5-ml spoon/½ teasp salt

Chop the chicken pieces into manageable sizes and put them into a large, deep saucepan or stock-pot of 3½–4½ litres/6–8 pints/4–5 quarts capacity. Cover well with water, bring the water slowly to the boil and skim thoroughly. Add the peeled carrots, peeled and halved onion, the stalk of celery, the parsley, bay, and thyme. Skim again as the water returns to the boil, add the salt, lower the heat, and half-cover the pot with a lid. Simmer for about 3 hours, topping up with water as necessary, and skimming frequently.

Strain the broth through a colander lined with 2–3 layers of cheesecloth or muslin, cool, and refrigerate, removing the fat – which will rise and solidify at the top – when ready to use.

Meat broth

Make as for the chicken broth, using, say 360 g/12 oz shin (fore shank) of mature beef and 720 g/1½ lb very meaty veal bones chopped by the butcher into manageable sizes – or if veal is unavailable, a large fleshy chicken carcass – plus chopped chicken pieces and the same vegetal ingredients and salt, with a large unpeeled garlic clove thrown in. Use the same size pot, about the same amount of water, and simmer half-covered for 4–5 hours, topping up with water and skimming as you see fit.

If you want a broth of good deep colour, such as that required for the *sauces vin rouge* and *poivre vert* on pages 43–4, first brown the beef, bones, and vegetables in a roasting pan in a hot oven, pour fat from the pan, deglaze it with water, put all into the stock-pot, cover with the requisite litres/pints/quarts of water, and proceed as above.

Fish broth

To make about 1½ litres/2½ pints/6 cups.

1400 g/3 lb bones and heads from
    lean fish such as sole, whiting,
    turbot, plaice, lemon sole,
    flounder, red snapper, or
    whatever is appropriate to you
2 leeks

1 large onion
8 or so parsley stalks
60 ml/4 tbs lemon juice
2 large glasses dry white wine, plus
    more at the end
One 2.5-ml spoon/½ teasp salt

Wash the fish bones and heads of all blood and discard the gills. Chop bones into convenient sizes and put them into a large, deep saucepan or stock-pot of 3½–4½ litres/6–8 pints/4–5 quarts capacity with the cleaned, chopped leeks, peeled and chopped onion, parsley, and lemon juice. Cover well with water, bring the water to the simmer, skim thoroughly, add the wine and salt and simmer, uncovered, for half an hour.

Strain the broth through a colander lined with 2–3 layers of cheesecloth or muslin, add a few drops of white wine to refresh the broth's flavour, let it cool, and refrigerate until needed.

A versatile vinaigrette

Red or white wine vinegar
French mustard, Dijon if possible
Cloves of garlic
Salt and pepper

Castor (granulated) sugar
Olive oil
Fresh herbs if you like

This is a procedure for which we rarely measure anything, preferring to rely on eye and frequent tasting to determine quantities.

So start by putting, say 15 ml/1 tbs of vinegar in a small bowl, add a generous 15-ml spoon/generous tbs of mustard, 1 or 2 cloves of garlic (bruised, peeled, and broken down with salt – under a small knife blade – to a paste) if you like garlic, liberal amounts of salt and pepper, and a 2.5-ml spoon/$\frac{1}{2}$ teasp of sugar. Whisk all these together with a fork and slowly pour on the olive oil. The mustard will cause the ingredients to emulsify.

After adding what you judge to be about five 15-ml spoons/5 tbs of oil, stop and taste. At this point we usually put in more mustard and seasoning, and sometimes more garlic. The ideal is very well-seasoned but not too acid – the vinegar can be replaced by lemon juice if you like, but its character in such small quantity gets rather lost under the impact of other ingredients. The sugar – actually very little – gives an interesting dimension to the flavour, and remember that the total effect will be lessened when coating heaps of leaves.

You can start out with double or triple these quantities in roughly the same proportions, and when you have made enough dressing and like its character, stop adding things and whisk the mixture vigorously, tossing in some fresh chopped herbs if you choose. If you don't add the herbs, the vinaigrette can be stored, tightly-covered, for days in the refrigerator. Bring it to room temperature and whisk well before use.

Three basic pastries

Shortcrust I
A touch of sugar gives this pastry good colour and a special accent. The dough holds its shape well and is excellent for quiches.

Makes enough to line a 23 cm/9 in flan ring, plus several small tarts.

240 g/8 oz/generous 1½ cups plain
    flour
A good pinch of salt (unless butter
    is salted)

One 15-ml spoon/1 tbs icing
    (confectioners') sugar
150 g/5 oz soft butter, unsalted if
    possible
1 egg

Sift together the flour, salt if used, and sugar onto a large pastry board, make a well in the centre, put butter into the well, make a trough in the butter and carefully break in the egg. With the fingers of one hand, work the egg and butter into a sticky mass. Wash your hand and use a spatula or palette knife to toss and chop the flour into the mass until pastry starts to form. Bring this together with both hands, add a few drops of water if necessary to make it adhere, knead briefly and form into a ball. Wrap the ball in greaseproof or waxed paper and a plastic bag and refrigerate for several hours or overnight.

Bring the dough to room temperature before rolling it out.

Shortcrust II
This is a sweetier, crumblier, and slightly nutty pastry, due to a greater quantity of sugar and the addition of ground almonds and 2 hard-boiled egg yolks. Makes enough for two 23 cm/9 in flan rings.

300 g/10 oz/2 cups plain flour
A good pinch of salt (unless butter
    is salted)
Two 15-ml spoons/2 tbs ground
    almonds

60 g/4 tbs castor (granulated)
    sugar
180 g/6 oz soft butter, unsalted if
    possible
Sieved yolks of 2 hard-boiled eggs
1 raw egg

Make this shortcrust exactly as the first, sifting together the 4 dry ingredients and sprinkling the sieved yolks into the trough in the butter before adding the egg. Wrap and refrigerate in the same way.

Puff pastry

Americans and other cooks whose plain "all-purpose" flour is stronger than the British, Australian, South African, etc. equivalents may want to replace 60 g/2 oz/a scant ½ cup of the plain flour with bleached cake flour in order to make the pastry more workable.

Yields about 1400 g/3 lb pastry.

480 g/1 lb/3½ cups plain flour
One 2.5-ml spoon/½ teasp salt
(unless butter is salted)

540 g/18 oz firm butter, unsalted
if possible
About 240 ml/8 fl oz/1 cup cold
water

Sift the flour and salt, if used, into a bowl, cut 90 g/3 oz of the butter into cubes and rub these into the flour, or cut them in with two knives. Pour in enough water to bind the ingredients – you may need the full amount but don't add it all until you've seen how much the flour will take – make the pastry into a ball, and knead it vigorously on a floured board for 5 minutes. This dough is called in French the *détrempe*. Make a ball of it again, wrap it in greaseproof or waxed paper and refrigerate to relax for an hour.

Put the remaining butter between two pieces of greaseproof or waxed paper and use a rolling pin to beat it into a slab of 13–15 cm/5–6 in square. Wrap and keep it cool – if necessary in the lowest part of the refrigerator.

After the *détrempe* has rested, flour the pastry board and roll the dough into a circle or square, keeping it slightly thicker in the middle than at the sides, place the butter in the centre, fold the *détrempe* over the butter to enclose it completely and seal the dough with your fingers. Turn it over.

Flour board and pastry and roll the dough into a rectangle of about 40 cm/16 in long by 20 cm/8 in wide, fold it into three from bottom to top like a business letter, give it a 90° turn so that one open end of the "letter" is toward you, and flour it if necessary. Roll the pastry again into a rectangle, fold it into three once more, make two slight dents in the side of the dough with your fingers to indicate it has had two turns, and chill it for an hour.

Give the pastry two more turns as above – always flouring if the butter starts to break through, or resting it in the refrigerator if the dough gets recalcitrant or the butter too soft – then make four dents to indicate four turns, wrap the pastry airtight and chill it overnight.

When ready to use, cut off the weight you need and give the puff its final pair of turns before rolling it out.

Coffee afterwards

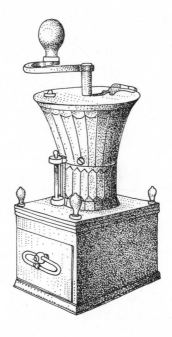

We yield to none in our partiality to a *demitasse* of rich Mysore, or the suave blend of roasts that is known as Vienna; but an imaginative menu deserves an original epilogue, and you may consider foamy iced coffee if the weather is right – or, if contrary, a steaming *Mexicana* of strong coffee liaised with chocolate and topped with cream, cinnamon and nutmeg. *Café Sevillano* is an intriguing alternative: bring the zest of 3 oranges plus 3 small spoons of granulated sugar to the boil in a pint or so of water. Strain, make the coffee with this brew, and float thick cream on top. New Orleans *brûlé* and Gaelic coffee have their following, but we find that most of the other spirited concoctions taste too strongly of their liqueur.

Balzac, who blended beans from three different Paris merchants, claimed that coffee caused ideas for his novels "to advance in columns en route like battalions of the *grande armée*". Pope Clement VIII declared the beverage good for the soul, and others believe (perhaps in the spirit of the Spanish Inquisition) that ultimate bliss can be achieved only through the correct degree of roasting. Jordanian bedouins maintain that grilling the beans over a fire of camel dung brings out their total flavour, but none of our testers has reported on this.

Seven years after the death of its founder André Simon, the Wine & Food Society celebrated his hundredth birthday. A committee of his friends met to decide on the menu he would most have enjoyed. There was much argument, but unanimity on one point: the great gastronome's ideal postscript to a fine meal was – a double helping of coffee ice cream.

Index

References are given under the name of the recipe, the type of dish (eg: main-course dishes, soups, etc.), and the principal ingredients. The latter are usually given under their English names; for alternatives see the *Note to cooks* on pp. xviii–xxii